Ignite The Fire Within!

It Only Takes A Moment To Change Your Life

Arthur J. Johnson II

PRESS

To Pam,

God Bless You!

2 Timothy 1:6

Arthur J. Johnson

7-31-04

Dedication

This book is dedicated to my loving wife, Artavia, who is not only my wife but also my best friend. Thank you for believing and keeping the faith! Your devotion, love and unfailing support made this book a reality. And to my loving son, Joshua, my computer companion, thank you!

Acknowledgments

I'd like to say thank you to:

My Lord and Savior Jesus Christ for truly making all things possible. You are awesome and the sole source from which true salvation, strength and success flow!

My loving wife, Artavia, for her untiring encouragement, love, patience and support throughout the writing of this book. I'm ever mindful and grateful for the sacrifices you made to help bring this book to pass. I couldn't have done it without you. Thank you.

My mom, dad, sister and brother for their constant love and encouragement. Your unwavering belief and support has made all the difference. You've always been there. This one is for you.

My mother-in-law, extended family and friends for loving me, supporting me and believing in all I've done.

My editor, Elaine Reeder Mayo, for her patience and editing expertise as we read, reviewed and edited the manuscript. I'm indebted to you for your tireless dedication and devotion to this project. Your assistance was invaluable; I couldn't have done it without you.

The many people I've had the privilege and pleasure to share words of insight, inspiration and motivation. Your countless words of encouragement and thanks have been priceless and have provided the inspiration needed for the writing of this book, which for me has been a labor of love.

Those who read this book. I encourage you to ignite your fire and seize your moments! Take action. It's your life and your legacy. Don't leave it to chance. And never give up on yourself, your desires and your dreams for a better tomorrow, no matter what! It's one of the greatest treasures you have to live for and look forward to.

Preface

Inspiration is a powerful phenomenon! It can lift you up, get you going and keep you going. My overwhelming desire and purpose in life is to help and inspire people to live productive, purposeful and successful lives. To succeed at home, in the workplace and in virtually every area of life. The words on the following pages are the result of me endeavoring to fulfill my life's purpose.

How It All Started

I was blessed and fortunate to be selected to join an awesome medical center management team as its Finance Manager. Prior to my arrival, this group of star performers had just opened a multimillion-dollar medical center. They had reached the pinnacle. The peak of accomplishment! It was during my first management meeting that I was asked to share a few words. What a significant moment – the opportunity to address a group of superachievers. I briefly spoke on the wise words of Solomon when he said, "If you faint in the day of adversity, your strength is small." Truly, they had come together, persevered and produced the winning prize. Those words spoke to the spirits of individuals in the room. After the meeting, I was asked to send out daily email messages with words of inspiration. I seized the moment – a divine appointment to exercise my purpose and maximize my potential!

I had no idea the enormous impact these messages would have on others. People began sending emails sharing how various messages had impacted and inspired them. I was truly humbled by this experience. A few of the comments are below:

- *"Art, you probably will never fully know how much these messages have touched each member of the management team at different points in our journey over the last year. I know God meant for you to be here and I am so glad we are blessed to work with you."*

- *"I want so much to achieve excellence, to do something really GREAT! I am learning however, that I am required to first be faithful over the little things, then and only then will GOD trust me with GREATNESS!"*

- *"I am speechless! Your husband writes so very well. I truly believe that he is in tune with our Father. Please encourage him to continue! His messages are truly a blessing to me. Thanks for sharing! Keep them coming!"*

- *"I just love getting your e-mails. I so appreciate you sending them to me. I've decided to start my own business and each time I get down on myself, one of your great messages pops up! They help keep my spirits up and my determination gets strengthened each and every time. Thank you so much!"*

- *"Thank you! You provide me much inspiration at such appropriate times. Words that really make me examine myself. I will be a better person at work and at home because I have the opportunity to work with you. I am very blessed."*

- *"Spiritual messages come at such appropriate times. He truly is with me each and every second. I had just encountered what I considered an impossible situation for today and then I opened this e-mail. It's possible now. Everything is possible!"*

- *"I let yesterday go without saying Thank You but today I can not do it...Thank You, Thank You, Thank You...once again God has used you in a mighty way."*

- *"Thanks. It is going to be the best year yet! My wife and I are communicating better than ever. We are finally working together and communicating daily regarding finances. Again, thanks for your prayers and help."*

- *"I know I haven't told you lately what a blessing you are to me and my spiritual well-being. Thank you and God Bless you and yours."*

- *"Thank you so much for this! This addresses an issue that is heavy on my heart and has been frightening. I cannot understand God's purpose in this, but now I will read Deuteronomy and what you've written, and keep praying."*

- *"Mr. Johnson I wanted you to see how you are blessing people you don't even know...keep on being obedient because you are helping to change lives."*

—*"Thank you so much for sharing the inspirational messages with me from Mr. Johnson! It's such a blessing to have someone devote their time and energy in reaching out to encourage people. At certain times in my life, I received those messages as 'right now' words for me. Not only did they encourage and inspire me, but I was able to pass the word on to those around me. They too appreciated it greatly. If you get a chance, let Mr. Johnson know that his labor has definitely not been in vain. People indeed need a boost from time to time in order to help propel them into their destiny. People need to be reminded to continue to move forward, especially in the things of God. I am just glad that Mr. Johnson yielded to his calling to admonish the people. God chose a wonderful vessel to use for His glory. God bless!"*

—*"I LOVE the emails you sent, my co-workers have me send them on our group email list. Sometimes when we take our lunch break together we discuss the topics that you send. These topics cause my co-workers to do some Bible study, and a lot of them don't go to church."*

—*"Everything you have sent me has blessed my heart and soul. I have also been sending them to others. Tell him thanks a lot. May God bless him."*

• *"Art, Thank you for your kind, inspirational words. I look forward to seeing them and aspire to practice them. I just haven't taken the time to thank you for them lately and want you to know what a joy your messages are."*

In addition to receiving words of encouragement and

thanks, I started receiving emails from individuals asking to be added to the daily email list. Unbeknownst to me, the messages were being sent to others. The words of inspiration and motivation were traveling far and wide!

Several people began encouraging me to write a book so that others could be inspired and motivated in the same way. Once again, I seized the opportunity and what you're reading is a result of that opportunity being maximized!

My desire is that the words on the following pages will do for you what they've done for so many others – *Ignite The Fire Within!*

Arthur J. Johnson

Contents

GET INSPIRED

and

Ignite The Fire Within!

For this reason I remind you to fan into flame the gift of God, which is in you . . .
2 Timothy 1:6

Introduction

Is your life overflowing with achievement, greatness, happiness and success? Do you sense there is more to life for you? In fact, you know there's more for you. Better health, better relationships, more joy, more love, more money, more promotions and more success. I couldn't agree with you more! There is more to life for you, but it will not just show up.

You must focus on what you really want every moment of your life and take action. Tremendous action! Your focus is determining your future, just as your decisions are determining your direction, which is ultimately leading you to your destination. Your destiny!

Are you going in the right direction? Will you reach your destination? Every moment, every second, counts. Seize it! Focus on your desires, dreams and goals, take action and your life will be an adventure filled with achievement and success. Every waking moment!

Ignite The Fire Within – It Only Takes A Moment To Change Your Life is a series of inspiring and motivating messages written to empower you to become more, do more and have more. To live the life you were created to live! A life filled with achievement and success. It's your birthright! What you have experienced in life is a result of who you are; and if you want more, you must become more. You have to work on your greatest asset. You! If you get better, things get better; if you change, things change. It's all about you!

Your future and your life are too valuable to be left to chance. Life is not a matter of chance, but a matter of choice; you increase your chances by making *inspired* choices.

They are the creators of your destiny. In the famous words of William Jennings Bryan, "Destiny is not a matter of chance, it is a matter of choice; it is not a thing to be waited for, it is a thing to be achieved." Don't wait any longer. It's time!

Don't be guilty of sitting around waiting for something to happen. When the inspiration hits – and it will – go with it! Follow it. Seize it! Take action and make something happen!

Know that you have everything you need right now, at this present moment, to get everything you want from life. To be a total success in all you do! Tap into it; it's inside of you. Don't just prepare to live; at some point, you have to live! Get inspired, and make every moment and every second of your life count.

The seconds are silently slipping away, to never return again. Get started on your path to *Ignite The Fire Within – It Only Takes A Moment To Change Your Life*! It truly only takes a moment to change your life. Do it . . . now!

You Can Make It Happen!

*Whatever your hand finds to do, do it with
all your might.*
— Ecclesiastes 9:10

*I know the price of success: dedication, hard
work and an unremitting devotion to the
things you want to see happen.*
— Frank Lloyd Wright

Use What You Have!

Then the Lord said to him, "What is that in your hand?"
"A staff," he replied.
– Exodus 4:2

From a little spark may burst a mighty flame.
– Dante Alighieri

Are you waiting for the perfect set of circumstances to get started? Maybe you're waiting for this to happen or that to happen before you get started, before you start living. Wait no longer. Time doesn't wait and you shouldn't either.

Peter Marshall said, "Let us not be content to wait and see what will happen, but give us the determination to make the right things happen." I know you can make it happen! The question is, "Will you?" Will you use what you have to get what you want? Everything you need to be a success, you already have! It just needs to be acknowledged, appreciated and celebrated.

This great leader in Exodus had a tremendous task

ahead, and felt he didn't have what was needed. You may be going through the same thing. But, fortunately he did have all he needed. And so do you! Listen . . . all you have is all you need, and all you need is all you have. Just use it! His success was in his hands the entire time. And so is yours!

He held the tool that would turn his dreams and goals into a reality. You are no different. Your success is in your hands, but you must realize it and recognize it. Tap into your success mindset and use your tools. You must know that you were born to win and created to succeed. Rise up to your potential and use all your resources.

What you need may not physically be in your hand, but it's definitely in your head and in your heart. Use it! If you use your head and your heart, you can be anything, create anything and do anything imaginable. The key is to use what you have. Do something. You either use it or lose it. Don't let what you do not have stop you from using and maximizing what you do have. If you're not using what you have, how can you ever expect to get more? Use what you have and watch everything else take care of itself. Do it!

Start by doing what's necessary, then what's possible, and suddenly you are doing the impossible.
– Saint Francis of Assisi

Though thy beginning was small,
yet thy latter end should greatly increase.
– Job 8:7

It's Time To Do It!

Do not merely listen to the word, and so deceive
yourselves. Do what it says.
– James 1:22

*To always be intending to live a new life, but never to find
time to set about it; this is as if a man should put off eating
and drinking and sleeping from one day and night to
another, till he is starved and destroyed.*
– Tillotson

Don't deceive yourself any longer. It's now or never! If
not now, when? If not you, then who? Your future is
all about you. What are you waiting for? You have everything you neèd. It's all inside. Look within. It's time to go
after your desires, dreams and goals. You've talked about it
and talked about it. Don't you think it's time to start walking
in your destiny? I think so!

John Wanamaker remarked, "One may walk over the
highest mountain one step at a time." Was he talking about
you? I believe he was. It's time to step out, step over and

step up! It's time to do it.

It has been said that inch-by-inch anything is a cinch. Do you believe that? The key is to be doing something. To be making progress, no matter how large or small. Are you making progress? Measure your results. Even if it's an inch, it's better than nothing. It gets you started and out of the gate. And once you take the first step, the second step is almost automatic. Ever watch a baby take his first step? It's almost instinct to take the next one.

But many of us have deceived ourselves into believing that if we just talk about it and think about it, miracles will happen. Not true! Miracles happen by taking action. By doing. Take action and start your miracle process. Work your own miracle. Do what you know you can do.

Stop talking and start walking; stop thinking and start doing. You already know what to do and how to do it. Now is the time to do it. And even if you don't, act like you do and it will come to you. Don't wait any longer . . . it may just be too late. Do it. Now!

Knowing is not enough, we must apply.
Willing is not enough, we must do.
– Johann von Goethe

The great end of life is not knowledge, but action.
– Thomas Henry Huxley

Check Your Results!

By their fruit you will recognize them.
– Matthew 7:16

Success is dependent on effort.
– Sophocles

When is the last time you checked your numbers? Bank account balance, books read, current salary, weight gain or weight loss. Numbers tell the story. They tell the factual story, but they don't necessarily tell the final story. You control that! What will your final story be? A story of achievements or disappointments, successes or failures? You are creating your destiny with every choice you make.

What type of results have you been producing? Are you satisfied with them? If not, why not? Or do you know that you're capable of producing more than you've been producing? Well if this is true, now is the time to start doing more. Refuse to wait any longer. Begin today, and you're bound to make it to the top!

Andrew Carnegie, one of the richest men to ever live,

commented in his later years, "As I grow older, I pay less attention to what men say. I just watch what they do." Are you paying attention to what's being said or what's being done? The results are in the doing!

Don't let opportunity and success pass you by. It's okay to say things, but after everything is said and done, there must be action. Action is what produces results. Not mere talk! And every action causes a reaction. What type of reactions have you been experiencing? Produce results, not regrets!

Jesus, the wise teacher said, "You will know them by their fruits." Not by what they say, but the actions they produce. What are you known by: your actions or your words? An old proverb says, "Doing is better than saying." Another says, "Saying is one thing, and doing another." Again, what are you known by?

Are you a person who perseveres because of, and succeeds in spite of, setbacks and situations? There are four types of people: those who watch what happens; those who wonder what happened; those who don't know what happened and those that make things happen. What category are you in? Are you making things happen? Someone is depending on you, and you should be depending on yourself. If you can't count on you, whom can you count on? You can make it happen!

Nothing worthwhile comes easily. Half effort does not produce half results, it produces no results. Work, continuous work and hard work, is the only way to accomplish results that last.
– Hamilton Holt

Striving for success without hard work is like trying to harvest where you haven't planted.
– David Bly

It's In The Doing!

Anyone, then, who knows the good he ought to do
and doesn't do it, sins.
— James 4:17

In putting off what one has to do,
one runs the risk of never being able to do it.
— Charles Baudelaire

What is it that you know you should be doing? Eating less, exercising more, saving regularly, spending less? Are you doing it or just thinking about it? Listen! Nothing happens until you do something. It's not enough just to know about success, you have to do successful things. Develop "success habits" and then make success a habit. It's good to think, but it's even better to take action on what you think. This is what produces results!

Are you a person of action? One who gets things done and makes things happen? Question: are there areas in your life where you know you can do better and should do better? What are you waiting for? Get up and get going!

Do what needs to be done.

Thomas Henry Huxley said, "The rung of a ladder was never meant to rest upon, but only to hold a man's foot long enough to enable him to put the other somewhat higher." You've rested long enough. It's time to step up to the next level. It's okay to rest, but make sure you don't rest too long. Don't confuse a rest stop with your final stop, your destination. You're not there yet. There is more!

There's more to be, more to do, more to give and more to have. But you have to act on it. You have to make it happen. And you can! You know what to do, you just need to do it! Break through those self-imposed limitations and operate in the "no limit" realm. There truly are no limits – only those you conceive and believe.

Don't delay! If you know you can do better, then do better. If you know you should do better, then do better. Now! Wherever you are, get started; whatever you have, use it. Why wait? Why would you not do what you know you could do? This only leads to failure – failure in a grand fashion. And I know you're not a failure. What are you going to do?

Even if you're on the right track,
you'll get run over if you just sit there.
– Will Rogers

Begin doing what you want to do now.
– Marie Beynon Ray

What's Your Plan For Success?

The plans of the diligent lead to profit as surely
as haste leads to poverty.
— Proverbs 21:5

*Where no plan is laid, where the disposal of time is
surrendered merely to the chance of incident,
chaos will soon reign.*
— *Victor Hugo*

There are many things desired in life. Great careers,
great family, great health and even great wealth. Will
they ever be a reality or just a figment of the imagination?
The answer to this inviting question lies in the plan that has
been developed to achieve these things. We're all too familiar with the saying, "People don't plan to fail; they just fail
to plan!" I'm a firm believer that things don't just happen,
but they do happen just.

Prior planning does prevent poor performance! Have

you ever tried to do something without a plan? Try going to the grocery store without a list (plan). You end up spending more than you wanted and bringing home things you probably didn't need. Be truthful! The truth will set you free. It will set you free to make corrections in previous errors in judgment. Without a plan, the only alternative is impulse! Be led by purpose, not impulse. The view is much better.

A good plan and disciplined effort produces success. Solomon calls it profit. He also warns that haste leads to poverty. Are you experiencing profit or poverty in your finances, your health, your relationships? He's basically saying that operating with no plan leads to no measurable progress. Without a plan, you're tossed with the wind and controlled by circumstance.

Don't be a victim of failing to plan. Behind every success is a plan for success. Plan your success and work your plan! What does your plan look like? Your career plan, your financial plan, your health plan, your wealth plan. Is it leading you to your ideal destination?

Take a good look! Your plan is making you or breaking you, working for you or working against you. Which is it? Hopefully it's working for you and creating continual profits and permanent success!

Before everything else,
getting ready is the secret of success.
– Henry Ford

The successful person is the individual who forms
the habit of doing what the failing person
doesn't like to do.
– Donald Riggs

Are You Prepared
To Succeed?

The horse is made ready for the day of battle,
but victory rests with the Lord.
— Proverbs 21:31

*The secret to success in life is for a man
to be ready for his opportunity when it comes.*
— Benjamin Disraeli

Fulfilled desires, dreams and goals are reserved for the prepared. The ones who are willing to work when no one is watching and labor when no one is looking. Is that you? Are you preparing for success and significance? Are you doing the positive things necessary to ensure a positive outcome? Success happens one act at a time, one day at a time. Just as preparation does. It's an ongoing process. Are you prepared?

If we practice success habits, we will make success a habit. It's really that simple. You're probably familiar with the "5-P" saying, "Prior Preparation Prevents Poor Performance!" It still holds true in every area of our lives.

B.C. Forbes asserted, "Opportunity can benefit no man who has not fitted himself to seize it and use it. Opportunity woos the worthy, shuns the unworthy. Prepare yourself to grasp opportunity, and opportunity is likely to come your way. It is not so fickle, capricious and unreasoning as some complain." Opportunity is on its way whether you're ready for it or not. And since you know its coming, why not be prepared to maximize it?

It just makes good sense. Don't you agree?

Solomon amazes us with his insight and instruction! He basically tells us that we have a responsibility to prepare. Prepare for what? Opportunity! But guess what? Success rests with the Lord. What a partnership! We are not in it alone.

If we prepare, it just seems like we summon other positive forces to act on our behalf. If we push back from the table and walk around the block, the body begins to partner with us and cooperate with our weight loss plans. If we start a little earlier and stay a little later, it just seems like things always work out for the greater good. It works!

Being prepared is the key! Remember these words: it's better to be prepared and never have an opportunity, than to have an opportunity and not be prepared! The irony is that if you prepare, you will attract the success opportunity you've prepared for. Progress and success are reserved for the prepared!

Know thine opportunity.
– Pittacus

The successful man is one who had the chance and took it.
– Roger Babson

There's Nothing To It . . . But To Do It!

All hard work brings a profit, but mere talk
leads only to poverty.
— Proverbs 14:23

*In putting off what one has to do,
one runs the risk of never being able to do it.*
— Charles Baudelaire

An anonymous person once stated these words and they are still true today: "Don't wait for your ship to come in, swim out to it." Are you waiting for something to happen? You've been dreaming about it and maybe even talking about it, but it's still not here. It still hasn't appeared. The desire, the dream, the goal is still out there somewhere. Could it be that you haven't been doing all that's necessary to create what you really want? Instead of waiting for it to happen, why not make it happen?

We are encouraged that in all hard work and labor there

is profit. There is gain; there is advantage. But it must be the right type of labor. Labor of action and not labor of talk! We are warned that mere talk and idle chatter only leads to poverty. It produces nothing! Instead of talking we need to be laboring. Doing! Making it happen.

Are you talking about your desires, dreams and goals or working on them? Are you talking about losing weight, or are you actually eating less and walking around the block for good health? It's all in the doing! I say do both, but make sure you are doing more working than talking. The labor will speak for itself. It will create a life of its own.

Labor is what produces. It produces life! New life, new joy, new hope and new inspiration. All because you did something. You did the right thing, the necessary thing. Any mother would agree that labor brings its share of pain, but the pleasure and joy of new life far outweigh the pain of labor.

Stop talking and start doing. There is nothing to it . . . but to do it!

Putting off an easy thing makes it hard.
Putting off a hard thing makes it impossible.
– George Claude Lorimer

If you want to do something, do it!
– Plautus

It's Time To Take Off!

As the body without the spirit is dead,
so faith without deeds is dead.
— James 2:26

If you want to do something, do it!
— Plautus

Reality is the name of the game. You must act on what you believe! Nothing happens until you act. No action, no reaction. Your desires, dreams and goals will never materialize unless you take off. You must back them up with action!

If you don't take action, your desires, dreams and goals will sit on the runway of your mind and ultimately get run over by doubt, fear, hesitation and procrastination. What a tragic scene! "I should do better, could do better, and don't do better." A catastrophic disaster waiting to happen!

Douglas Everett asserted, "There are some people who live in a dream world, and there are some who face reality; and then there are those who turn one into the other." Which one are you? Are you turning your dreams into reality or living in a dream world of denial? Face the facts and act. It's time to wake up and take it up to another level. Today is a new day, and you have a date with destiny. Your plane and your life are on the runway.

It's time to take off on your dreams! Can you imagine an airplane sitting on a runway and never taking off? Senseless! It will never reach its destination. Many of us want to go places in life, but we won't take off. We won't push the throttle on life.

Don't be afraid of change, progress and success. It's all part of the game of life. If you don't push forward, you won't move forward. You either live life or life lives you. You either act on life or life acts on you. Which will it be? The tower is waiting for a response!

Something has to happen!
– Heinrich Boll

Act decidedly and take the consequences.
No good is ever done by hesitation.
– Thomas Henry Huxley

Your Attitude Makes The Difference!

I can do everything through him
who gives me strength.
– Philippians 4:13

Nothing can stop the man with the right
mental attitude from achieving his goal;
nothing on earth can help the man
with the wrong mental attitude.
– W.W. Ziege

A New Attitude . . .
A New Altitude!

Then this Daniel was preferred above the presidents and princes, because an excellent spirit was in him; and the king thought to set him over the whole realm.
– Daniel 6:3 (KJV)

Our belief at the beginning of a doubtful undertaking is the one thing that ensures the successful outcome of our venture.
– William James

What are your thoughts and feelings like? Do you think it's time for an attitude adjustment? A new attitude! Attitude is to success, as yeast is to bread. Without it, your chances of rising or slim to none. It doesn't matter whether you're trying to get out of debt, launch a new career, loose weight or salvage a broken relationship, attitude is the key to your success.

Check your attitude! It's either causing you to rise or

keeping you down. There's no middle of the road. It's been said that attitude is a small thing that makes a big difference. Attitude is simply a state of thought or feeling. So if you're striving for something different, it's going to take a different attitude.

Albert Einstein observed, "The problems that exist in the world today cannot be solved by the level of thinking that created them." Change your attitude and increase your altitude. Don't let your attitude be affected by external circumstances and conditions. This is the one thing that you have control over. Your attitude! Don't loose control.

And yes, your attitude does determine your altitude! It's hard to go up, with a down attitude. Just as it's very hard to go down, with an up attitude. Take the high road and stay on top. Snap out of the low-level thinking! Low-level thinking doesn't produce high-level results!

Don't be your own worst enemy, but your best ally. Develop an attitude of excellence in all that you do. Why? Excellence reaps it's own rewards. Your attitude of excellence will not only affect you, but everything it comes into contact with. If you're not fully satisfied with your current results and rewards, check your attitude. It's a good gauge of your potential altitude!

Man's rise or fall, success or failure, happiness or unhappiness depends on his attitude... a man's attitude will create the situation he imagines.
– James Lane Allen

The greatest discovery of my generation is that man can alter his life simply by altering his attitude of mind.
– William James

A Can Do Attitude!

I can do everything through Him who gives me strength.
— Philippians 4:13

Man's rise or fall, success or failure,
happiness or unhappiness depends on his
attitude . . . a man's attitude will create
the situation he imagines.
— *James Lane Allen*

Do you have the belief that you can do anything? Why not? If you don't, you should. You are only limited by your inability to believe in yourself and what you have in you. You can do anything and everything, but it starts with having the right mental attitude.

Do you have that attitude? A "can do" attitude? Is there something you're trying to accomplish and it seems like nothing is working? Seems like it may never come to pass? Things might not work out? Don't loose hope! Keep working and telling yourself that you can do it, and it will work out. This one act will be one of the greatest factors of your future success. Telling yourself that "you can" in the face of your circumstances!

Henry Ford, the famous automaker, once spoke these words, "Whether you think you can or whether you think you can't, you're right!" Imagine that! You have the answer. The answer to your challenge and life's journey lies in what you're telling yourself. What have you been telling yourself?

We discover a great principle and truth. And that truth is that your "attitude" in the midst of a situation or circumstance is the one thing that will most positively or negatively impact the outcome of the situation. Paul was under house arrest, awaiting trial, and still espoused a "positive mental attitude." What type of attitude do you espouse in the face of challenge and struggle? Are you controlling your challenging situations or letting them conquer and control you?

He said I "can" do everything through Him who gives me strength. His belief created a "can do" attitude. Not his circumstance, but his belief. Focus on what you believe, not what you see, feel or experience! What do you believe? Do you believe you can? I believe you can!

And remember, it's okay to ask for help. We could all use a little help!

Immense power is acquired by assuring yourself in your secret reveries that you were born to control affairs.
– Andrew Carnegie

Nothing can stop the man with the right mental attitude from achieving his goal; nothing on earth can help the man with the wrong mental attitude.
– W.W. Ziege

Failure Is Not An Option!

He looked up and said, "I see people; they look like trees walking around." Once more Jesus put his hands on the man's eyes. Then his eyes were opened, his sight was restored and he saw everything clearly.
– Mark 8:24-25

If at first you don't succeed, try, try, try again.
– W. E. Hickson

What would you do if you knew you could not fail? The fear of failure often times keeps people from realizing their true potential and maximizing their performance. Are you facing this enemy of success?

Don't let the fear of failure destroy your dreams and goals. Tell yourself, "I can not fail and will not fail! Failure is not an option." No matter how things look on the outside, keep telling yourself that you can do it and keep on doing it.

George Matthew Adams asserted, "We can accomplish almost anything within our ability if we but think we can!" What you think determines what you do. Success really is an inside job! You may not get the right result the first time, but if you keep correcting and concentrating, correcting and concentrating, you will get the desired result and ultimately succeed. Guaranteed!

If you put forth an effort, you will always get a result. And if you keep trying and correcting, you will eventually get the desired result. The key is to keep trying! Jesus touched the blind man's eyes and got a result. But not the desired result. The man couldn't see clearly after the first touch; but Jesus possessed the "can't fail" attitude. He knew he could not fail, and so should you! So what did he do? He proceeded to touch the man eyes again, told him to look up and he was fully restored. You need to do the same thing.

Whatever it is you're doing, try again and look up. Go for the second touch and something will happen when you look up. Develop the "I can't fail" attitude and watch your personal and professional success soar to the next level. All because you knew you could not fail!

We would accomplish many more things if we
did not think of them as impossible.
– C. Malesherbez

Faith that the thing can be done is essential
to any great achievement.
– Thomas N. Carruther

Doing Better Than Your Best!

Remember that in a race everyone runs, but only one
person gets the prize. You also must run in such
a way that you will win.
– 1 Corinthians 9:24 (NLT)

*Fight one more round. When your feet are so tired you
have to shuffle back to the center of the ring,
fight one more round.*
– James J. Corbett

D o you have a "doing better than your best" philosophy? That is to say you're looking for constant and
consistent improvement. Some call it continuous improvement, but whatever it's called, the goal is to always "better
your best." Striving for total success in all that you do;
whether on the job or at home. Success and winning is the
aim. Second best is not an option!

We are reminded that life is sometimes like a race. We're

all doing something or going somewhere. We're in the action. But the real question is will you achieve your goal; will you make it to your destination? It all depends on your philosophy. The way you think. How do you feel about the race you're running? The life you're living? Are you in the right race? Are you living the life you desire and dream about?

We are encouraged to run and live in such a way as to win. That means that there is also a way that will result in losing. Are you winning or losing? Is there something that needs to change? Are you focused on the finish line or fleeing to the sideline?

Don't loose out and definitely don't miss out on life by fleeing to the sideline. This is your life, your time. Focus on the finish line. Why? Because wherever you focus is where you will finish. Focus on success and winning in all that you do and you will always do better than your best.

An unknown author penned these famous words: "He who does not hope to win has already lost!" I sure hope that you hope to win! See you at the finish line!

You go back to the gym and you just do it again
and again until you get it right.
– Arnold Schwarzenegger

You give 100 percent in the first half of the game,
and if that isn't enough, in the second half
you give what's left.
– Yogi Berra

Give It Your All!

Whatever your hands find to do, do it with all your might,
for in the grave, where you are going,
there is neither working, nor planning,
nor knowledge, nor wisdom.
    – Ecclesiastes 9:10

Do what you can, with what you have, where you are.
    – Theodore Roosevelt

What would life look like if you gave it your all? If everyday you chose to do no less than your best. If you gave all you had, and more, in everything you did. If you realized that it was your life and if it were going to be great, you would have to be the one to do it. If you took full responsibility for your life and the results you produced. Wouldn't life be a masterpiece? A work of art! Is this your current experience? If not, know that you can create it.

Maybe you need to develop the mindset of a sprinter. A sprinter gives 100 percent until he crosses the finish line. Not 95 percent, even 99 percent; 100 percent is the standard.

Why? Because there is always someone or something waiting in the shadow to steal the race and the ultimate victory. And that something is doubt, fear, neglect and procrastination. Don't let these enemies steal your victory.

What are you battling? Are you in competition with these dream killers and destiny stealers? If so, run right pass them! Don't slack up, and by all means, don't slow up. Give it your all until the very end. You want to be so far ahead in life that you are never behind. So far on top, that you're never at the bottom.

Frank Tyger noted, "Your future depends on many things, but mostly on you." Based on that, whatever you do, do it with all that you have in you. Don't settle for less than your best. It leads to less. Doing less than your best will corrupt your courage and crash your confidence! Whatever you do, give it your all. Your future is depending on you.

There will come a time when you won't be able to do what you can do now. Then what? Time is ticking away. The race has begun and will one day end. Where are you in your race? How far have you run? Are you still running or have you started jogging? Or maybe even walking. Wherever you are, take a deep breath, gain your second wind and get moving again. You only have one life to live. At least down here on Earth. Live it! Give it your all; give 100 percent until the very end.

May you live all the days of your life.
– Jonathan Swift

Most of us spend our lives as if we had
another one in the bank.
– Ben Irwin

What You Believe Determines What You Achieve!

Jesus said unto him, If thou canst believe, all things are possible to him that believeth.
– Mark 9:23 (KJV)

Our belief at the beginning of a doubtful undertaking is the one thing that ensures the successful outcome of our venture.
– William James

It's Time To Believe!

Jesus said unto him, If thou canst believe, all things are
possible to him that believeth.
– Mark 9:23 (KJV)

Some things have to be believed to be seen.
– Ralph Hodgson

Is there something you've been wanting and wishing for,
but it hasn't appeared yet? Could it be due to a lack of
belief? If you really want to check your belief, just
consider your actions. Action follows belief! You sit in
chairs, without even checking the durability and sturdiness
of the parts, because you believe it's going to hold you.
You don't even think twice about it; you just act. Why not
believe in your desires, dreams and goals the same way?
Just act on them. Start moving toward them and watch
them move closer to you.

Mary Kay Ash, an entrepreneur and pioneer in the direct
cosmetic sales industry, said, "Aerodynamically, the bumblebee shouldn't be able to fly, but the bumblebee doesn't know

it so it goes on flying anyway." In other words the bumblebee believes it can fly, so it goes on flying without any regard for physical conditions or physical limitations. What about you?

If a bumblebee has the good sense and savvy to ignore its shortcomings and play to its strengths, why not you? I'm sure it travels a lot farther flying, than walking. And so can you! Maximize your strengths and minimize your weaknesses. Do what you do best and leave the rest alone. Believe in yourself, plan to win and then play to win. Be smart and strategic and let your strengths lead the way!

You are only limited by your beliefs! In order to be more, do more and have more, you must believe for more. What are your current beliefs? I can't, or I can; I could never do that, or I will do that. You will have exactly what you're able to believe for. Nothing more, nothing less! If you don't believe it, you will never receive it. Why? Because you won't do what's necessary to make it happen.

Work on developing a new set of beliefs. Beliefs of action, faith, success and victory. Beliefs that will break through any setback and allow you to stage a major comeback. Why not believe and achieve?

We can accomplish almost anything within
our ability if we but think we can!
– George Matthew Adams

Faith that the thing can be done is essential
to any great achievement.
– Thomas N. Carruther

Get Started!

Whoever watches the wind will not plant;
whoever looks at the clouds will not reap.
— Ecclesiastes 11:4

Procrastination is opportunity's assassin.
— *Victor Kiam*

You've talked about it, thought about it and even wrote about it, but you haven't started yet. It seems like your life is on hold. Why? Know that nothing will happen until you take action! A starter visualizes the end and begins. Is that you? Do you have the mentality of a starter? He creates a picture of what he wants to be, do and have and goes to work on making it a reality. He puts the pieces together along the way. What does your picture look like? What are you waiting for to get started on your desires, dreams and goals? It's time!

Sydney Smith said, "To do anything in this world worth doing, we must not stand back shivering and thinking of the cold and danger, but jump in and scramble through as well as we can." Are you waiting for the perfect set of circumstances and conditions? Unfortunately, there probably won't be any; so it will be to your advantage and best interest to get started. Now! Don't miss your window of opportunity.

If you are waiting on something to happen outside of you, you will never get started. Nothing changes until you change; nothing gets better until you get better. What are you going to do? The clock has started, and time is ticking away!

Solomon observed, "He that observes the wind will not sow." In other words, if you are caught up with the circumstance, you will never take the chance necessary to break free. You will always be in neutral. He then says, "He that regards the clouds will not reap." If you're waiting for a sunny, perfect day to start out; you will always be stuck. Once again, you're in neutral, wanting to move forward, but in reality just moving in place. It's time to get started, move out and move up!

Don't look at what's around you. Look at what's in you and get started. Get moving . . . get going! Use all you have to become all you can become and to get all you want. It's your race; it's your life. Maximize it! Start living it to the fullest. Today is the perfect day.

No one should have to ask you, "When are you going to get started?" Maybe, "When are you going to slow down or stop?" but never, "When are you going to get started?"

Act decidedly and take the consequences.
No good is ever done by hesitation.
– Thomas Henry Huxley

If you want to do something, do it!
– Plautus

It's Time To Use What You Have!

A gift is as a precious stone in the eyes of him that hath it:
whithersoever it turneth, it prospereth.
– Proverbs 17:8 (KJV)

*Men take only their needs into consideration,
never their abilities.*
– Napoleon Bonaparte

You've been given a gift! Don't look for it. It's within
you. Just discover it, develop it and deploy it. At this
present moment, you have all that you need to be a total
success. To become all that you desire to be. All you need is
all you have, and all you have is all you need.

Your gift is what makes the difference. The question is,
"What will you do with this awesome treasure lying within
you?" Will you tap into it or leave it untapped? Tap into it. It
was given to you to be used, not to lie dormant.

Don't you think it's time to discover your gift, your

uniqueness and use it? Use what you have and get what you want. You can't expect more until you begin to use what you have. It just works out that way. If you use your gift, it will lift you to levels of success that you only dreamt about.

Coleman Fox quipped, "Even the woodpecker owes his success to the fact that he uses his head and keeps pecking away until he finishes the job he starts." To what do you owe your success? Or lack of success? Will you keep stretching until you reach success?

Is it that you're afraid to use what you have? Why? What you have is the key to your success. You will never know how great you can be if you don't use what you have. Someone once said, "You don't have to be great to get started, but you do have to get started to be great." Use what you have! Use your gift and watch it give you a lift. Your miracle begins in you. In your mind. Use it!

Everyone who got where he is had to begin where he was.
– Robert Louis Stevenson

We will not know unless we begin.
– Howard Zinn

It's Still Possible!

Then the disciples came to Jesus in private and asked,
"Why couldn't we drive it out?" He replied, "Because you
have so little faith. I tell you the truth, if you have faith as
small as a mustard seed, you can say to this mountain,
'Move from here to there' and it will move.
Nothing will be impossible for you."
– Matthew 17:19-20

Some things have to be believed to be seen.
– Ralph Hodgson

Have you been trying to do something but just haven't
been able to see it through? You've tried to make it
happen, but it just hasn't happened. Seems like nothing is
working. Keep on trying. Whatever you do, don't despair
and don't give up! If you give up, you will never go up!
Your true treasure will remain untouched!

Ask yourself the tough question and then tune in for the
answer. "Why haven't I done this? Why haven't I broken
through my limiting beliefs and changed careers, lost

weight, repaired broken relationships or started saving for the future? Why?"

The quality of your life will be determined by the quality of the questions that you ask yourself. What's keeping you from achieving success and reaching your goals? Is it you? Take responsibility. What's keeping you from turning impossibilities to possibilities? You hold the key. You are the answer you've been searching for. Success is in you. Just believe, receive and achieve!

Franklin Delano Roosevelt observed, "The only limit to our realization of tomorrow will be our doubts of today." He went on to say, "Let us move forward with strong and active faith." Could you be encountering an episode of disbelief and doubt? Lack of faith? You doubt yourself and your opportunities to be, do and have all that you want in life. If so, rid yourself of these self-sabotaging thoughts! They will stymie your progress and success everytime. Replace them with thoughts of belief and courage and take action. Massive action!

You must know and believe that you can do whatever you set your heart and mind to. Far too many people stop one second shy of success and one step away from stardom. Their own personal stardom! As long as you can believe it, you can achieve it and receive it. All things really are possible!

Faith sees the invisible, believes the incredible
and receives the impossible.
– Anonymous

Faith is to believe what we do not see; the reward of this
faith is to see what we believe.
– Saint Augustine

It's Not Over!

No, in all these things we are more than conquerors
through him who loved us.
– Romans 8:37

When the going gets tough, the tough get going.
– Frank Leahy

D o you feel like abandoning your dreams and hopes for
a better future? Don't do it! Your belief in the midst of
the battle is oftentimes the difference between winning and
losing. Don't give up on your desires and goals. They are far
too important!

Why would you even let a thought like that cross your
mind? Your desires and dreams represent who you are and
what you're capable of becoming. And remember winners
focus on finding ways to win! You were created to dominate!

Have you been living up to your potential? Have you been
dominating or have you been dominated? It's time for the
tides to turn. You've got to live up to your potential in order to
maximize your power. Your power is in your potential. But

you have to release it. If you don't live up to your potential, you lessen your power. You either use it or loose it. Have courage and use what you have to conquer and overcome the challenges and obstacles of life. It's not over until you succeed and win!

Listen! William Feather observed, "Success seems to be largely a matter of hanging on after others have let go." Have you let go? Are you willing to hang on until you succeed? This is what champions do. They hold on knowing that success and victory is sure to come. What about you? Are you a champion, a conqueror, an overcomer? Well then, hold on, conquer your challenge and create the life you dream about.

Don't let go of your dream for a better future! It's your dream to fulfill and only you can do it. Take charge and live up to your potential! Don't give up and just sit around waiting for something to happen or someone to come by and lift you up. What happens if they don't come? Get up! Stop sitting down on life. Stand up and live life like a champion, like an overcomer. Champions and conquerors do whatever it takes to win. Will you? It shouldn't be over until you win! What do you think? I thought you would agree!

To every disadvantage there is a corresponding advantage.
– W. Clement Stone

The greater the obstacle, the more glory in overcoming it.
– Moliere

You Can Do The Impossible!

Jesus looked at them intently and said,
"Humanly speaking, it is impossible. But not with God.
Everything is possible with God."
– Mark 10:27 (NLT)

*When you have a great and difficult task, something
perhaps almost impossible, if you only work a little at a
time, every day a little, suddenly the work will finish itself.*
– Isak Dinesen

Great news! You can do the impossible! Is there something you're trying to do or some place you're trying to
go and it doesn't seem like you're making progress? Well,
now is not the time to rest, and by all means don't give up.
Look up! If the outlook is bad, the up look is always good.

I found out that you can do the impossible! Yes, you can
do the impossible. Believe it, receive it and achieve it! The
key is to not try to do it yourself. The extra help is what

makes the difference! It's the difference between what looks impossible and what is actually possible. Ask for it!

Jesus looked at them very seriously and basically said, "Humanly speaking it is impossible. But not with God. With God everything is possible." What a promise! In other words, he was saying that in your own strength and power it is impossible. But there is a greater strength and power you can tap into if you want to do the impossible.

Are you striving for greatness? To do the extraordinary? To do what seems impossible to the natural eye? Well, in the presence of this great strength and power, impossibilities become possibilities. Obstacles become opportunities. And setbacks become stepping-stones to significance and success. There is no limit to your ability to achieve and succeed. Get in the power flow and do the impossible!

Do you want to do the impossible? Do you want to turn your desires and dreams into realities? Do you want to live a great life? A life filled with great accomplishments, achievements and affections? Well, you can if you're willing to take your seemingly impossibilities into the realm of limitless possibilities. Look up and take it up. Do it today. . . . take it to the next level!

It is by attempting to reach the top at a single leap that so much misery is caused in the world.
– William Cobbett

Yesterday I dared to struggle. Today I dare to win.
– Bernadette Devlin

The Best Is Yet To Come!

For I know the plans I have for you, declares the Lord,
plans to prosper you and not harm you,
plans to give you hope and a future.
– Jeremiah 29:11

When I look at the future, it's so bright, it burns my eyes.
– Oprah Winfrey

Does it seem like things aren't working? The plans you had aren't panning out. Goals you set have gone by the wayside. Dreams you dreamt are drowning in the doldrums of despair, discontent and doubt. Take notice! Today is a new day and your future is brighter than ever. Why? Someone once said, "Each day is like a blank sheet of paper. You can write whatever you want on it." What will you write about your day, your future?

You've been given all you need to succeed. You have to *believe* that because what you believe determines what you do! What do you believe about your future? Do you believe that the best is yet to come? You should! Why would you believe anything else? You'll get exactly what you expect to get. Your expectations attract. Expect the best!

Louis L' Amour said, "Everyone has it within his power to say, this I am today, that I shall be tomorrow." What have you been saying about your future? Don't be silent about your success. Speak it into existence! What you say, you begin to believe, and what you believe, you will eventually achieve and receive. Somehow, someway!

Question: "What do you believe about your future?" What will you become, what will you do, what will you have? You hold the key to your future! Use it. Unlock your potential and release your prosperity. Believe in yourself!

You are where you are today because of your beliefs; and you will be tomorrow where your beliefs lead you. Make sure you are headed in the direction of your destiny. If your current actions aren't supporting your future achievement, stop doing them. They're taking you in the wrong direction.

You can never get to the right place going the wrong way. Examine your beliefs about you and what you have going for you. You will be amazed at the great treasure within you. Tap into it! The best *is* yet to come! Believe it and receive it!

I like the dreams of the future better than
the history of the past.
– Thomas Jefferson

The future belongs to those who believe
in the beauty of their dreams.
– Eleanor Roosevelt

Don't Ever Stop Believing!

Then he touched their eyes and said,
"According to your faith will it be done to you;"
and their sight was restored.
– Matthew 9: 29-30

*Faith is to believe what you do not yet see;
the reward for this faith is to see what you believe.*
– *Saint Augustine*

Have you lost hope and stopped believing? Given up on your deepest desires, dreams and goals? Remember that what you believe determines what you see. Start believing again! It doesn't cost you anything but a change of attitude and a change of mind. Revive your quest for success and achievement!

Belief is a powerful thing. You can't do very much without it. Just ask the dieter who quit, the companion who gave up on the relationship, the person who settled for a life of poverty and pain. Every action, every reaction hinged on what they believed. They gave out and gave up. They stopped believing! Whatever you do, don't stop believing. It may be the only thing you have to hold on to. Don't let it go!

Ralph Hodgson remarked, "Some things have to be believed to be seen." Do you believe that? In other words, he's saying there are some things you won't see until you believe. Why? Because what you believe empowers you to break through the barriers to what you're able to achieve and receive. What do you really believe? Believe for the best! Believe in yourself and the rest will take care of itself!

Are you floundering in your finances, struggling in your situations, or wrestling with your weight because you haven't developed the belief that you can do it? Check your belief! It has been said that, "Faith sees the invisible, believes the incredible and receives the impossible." Believing unlocks the treasure chest of progress and success! Why not open yourself up to limitless opportunities?

What do you see for yourself? Today, tomorrow, in the future. What do you believe about you? Do you have what it takes to get what you want? The ability to achieve your goals, to receive the rewards of well thought out plans, acted on day after day. I believe you do! What about you?

Keep believing! It's the key to receiving!

Some things have to be believed to be seen.
– Ralph Hodgson

Faith is one of the forces by which men live;
the total absence of it means collapse.
– William James

Don't Let Doubt Take You Out!

Immediately Jesus reached out his hand and caught him.
You of little faith, he said, why did you doubt?
– Matthew 14:31

*To be ambitious for wealth, and yet always expecting to be
poor; to be always doubting your ability to get what you
long for, is like trying to reach east by traveling west.
There is no philosophy which will help a man to succeed
when he is always doubting his ability to do so, and thus
attracting failure. No matter how hard you work for
success, if your thought is saturated with the fear of failure,
it will kill your efforts, neutralize your endeavors
and make success impossible.*
– Charles Baudouin

Have you started to pursue your dreams and goals and gotten distracted along the way? You've taken your eye off the goal. Perhaps the vision of what you really wanted to be, do and have has fallen by the wayside. What happened?

Did you let fear and doubt creep in and cause confusion and delusion? Anytime you take your eye off the prize, you will be set back and sidetracked by these sideline enemies – disbelief, doubt, fear and negativity. You have to silence them! If you don't, they will keep you from walking in your destiny and living your dreams. This is why you have to stay focused on where you are going. If not, doubt will take you out! Replace doubt and fear with determination and faith and get back on track. Go for your goal. You can reach it!

William James, the prominent psychologist, proclaimed, "Our belief at the beginning of a doubtful undertaking is the one thing that ensures the successful outcome of the venture." Are you second-guessing your desires, dreams and goals? Why? What happened to the belief and enthusiasm you had at the beginning? The excitement and passion for progress and success? Refocus and reclaim it. It's still there.

Why allow your focus to falter? Focusing on the negatives rather than the positives will take you under every time. Doubt and negativity create fear, and unchecked fear leads to failure. Don't be controlled by your fears, but convinced and persuaded by your faith. Believe in your desires, dreams and goals. Believe in you!

Someone once said, "Fear knocked at the door. Faith answered. And lo, no one was there." Don't give in to your doubts and fears. Be determined, stay focused and conquer them. Don't let doubt and fear cause you to miss out. Your dreams and goals are too dynamic. Stay focused on what you want. And don't look to the left or to the right. Just look straight ahead. Keep your head up and your heart unmoved, and live life to the fullest!

A person who doubts himself is like a man
who would enlist in the ranks of his enemies
and bear arms against himself.
— Alexander Dumas

A man's doubts and fears are his worst enemies.
— William Wrigley, Jr.

Your Choices Create Your Consequences!

This day I call heaven and earth as
witnesses against you that I have set before
you life and death, blessings and curses.
Now choose life, so that you and
your children may live.
– Deuteronomy 30:19

Life is the sum of all your choices.
– Albert Camus

A New Resolution . . .
A New Result!

By the seventh day God had finished the work
he had been doing; so on the seventh day
he rested from all his work.
– Genesis 2:2

*Nothing worthwhile comes easily. Half effort does not
produce half results, it produces no results. Work,
continuous work and hard work, is the only way to
accomplish results that last.*
– Hamilton Holt

On January 1 of each year, many people launch out on what's called New Year's resolutions. Do you? They attempt to do things they didn't do the year before. For some strange reason, they stopped along the way. Does this sound familiar? Well, it's time to develop the habit of finishing what you start! Don't you agree? A new resolution produces a new result!

No more incomplete projects and unfulfilled promises. Do what you say you're going to do and don't stop until it's done. No matter what! Quitters never win, and winners never quit. When you make a commitment to believe and achieve, stopping is not an option. You have to execute and follow through until completion.

It's good to have starting power; but to see your desires and dreams come to life, you must have staying power . . . be willing to stick to your dreams and goals and see them through. If they are worth having, they have to be worth working for. No labor, no life! Labor produces life. Ask any mother; she would agree. Are you willing to work for what you desire and deserve? I hope so!

Listen! Horace Mann quipped, "I have never heard anything about the resolutions of the apostles, but a good deal about their acts." What are your daily actions like? Are they supporting your quest for success? You've heard the old saying, "Actions speaks louder than words." Are your actions speaking on behalf of your future success? Why not?

You must take action, everyday, on your desires, dreams and goals. Not every once in a while, but everyday! And don't rest until you've achieved your desired result. Why would you even think of stopping? Work is the essential ingredient. Keep on keeping on! Wishing and waiting won't win this one. It takes work! Real work!

Success is dependent on effort.
– Sophocles

In all human affairs there are efforts, there are results, and the strength of the effort is the measure of the result.
– James Lane Allen

Whose Side Are You On?

Jesus knew their thoughts and said to them, "Every kingdom divided against itself will be ruined, and every city or household divided against itself will not stand."
– Matthew 12:25

Your future depends on many things, but mostly on you.
– Frank Tyger

Do you ever wonder whose side someone is on? You can't really determine by his actions. He has on the same uniform, but his actions are suspect. He may even wear the same name, but something isn't right.

What about you? Are your actions lining up with your goals – the things you really want from life? Why not? You have to go *with* your goals. Not against them. You'll never achieve them if you're not going in the same direction. You'll always find yourself going against the current. Swimming upstream. Fighting an uphill battle. Get the picture!

Henry David Thoreau remarked, "I know of no more encouraging fact than the unquestionable ability of man to elevate his life by conscious endeavor." In other words, he's saying man has the ability to create the life he wants to live by taking "well thought out" action. Are your actions well thought out?

Financial struggles don't just surface, nor do extra pounds just show up. They are being summoned by every thought, every choice and every action you take. Have you been siding with success or failure? Just look at your actions. Why not distance yourself from those destructive attitudes and habits and side with destiny? It's the only way you will achieve your goals and make your life a stunning success!

Don't fight against who you really want to be any longer. Your body is asking for a banana, and you give it Boston cream pie. Your financial situation says stop spending, and you spend even more. Your health says walk around the block, and instead you walk to the refrigerator. Stop the insanity! Someone would say, "Whose side are you on?"

Whose side *are* you on? The side of success or the side of failure, the positive or the negative? The choice is yours! But know that your decision is determining whether your life goes to the next level or remains where it is. If nothing changes, everything remains the same. Whose side are you on?

A secure individual . . . knows that the responsibility for
anything concerning his life remains with himself –
and he accepts that responsibility.
– Harry Browne

He who would be well taken care of must
take care of himself.
– William Graham Sumner

What Choices Are You Making?

There is a way that seems right to a man,
but in the end it leads to death.
— Proverbs 14:12

Look for your choices, pick the best one,
then go with it.
— Pat Riley

Choices and consequences! Elizabeth Kubler-Ross commented, "I believe that we are solely responsible for our choices, and we have to accept the consequences of every deed, word, and thought throughout our lifetime." Do you believe that? Are you taking responsibility for your choices? Or does someone else get the blame? Don't play the blame game! You will loose every time.

Do you ever take time to truly evaluate your choices? That split-second that can make the difference between success and failure, victory and defeat. If not, begin today!

Don't make another choice without considering the consequences. Is it helping you or hindering you? Taking you forward or throwing you backwards? Change your choices and you change your life. It's that simple! Life doesn't have to be complex, but bad choices can make it that way.

Life is not a matter of chance, but a matter of choice. And you increase your chances, by making better choices. Are your choices aligned with your desires, dreams and destiny? Why are you making them? Are they empowering you or disempowering you, encouraging you or discouraging you? You don't have to settle for your current reality. There's more! And you have the power to choose it. Don't give away your power of choice! Make the positive choice.

There are choices that seem right in the beginning, but in the end, they don't produce. Stop making them! They are enemies to your success. Watch out for these choices. Choices like eating more than you need, spending more than you make and doing less than you can. Don't fall victim to these faulty choices. They will lead to the ultimate demise of your health plan, your financial plan and your success plan. Choose total success in all that you do. Make the right choice!

*We must make the choices that enable us to fulfill
the deepest capacities of our real selves.
– Thomas Merton*

*Choose always the way that seems the best,
however rough it may be; custom will soon render
it easy and agreeable.
– Pythagoras*

Make The Right Choice!

This day I call heaven and earth as witnesses against
you that I have set before you life and death,
blessing and curses. Now choose life,
so that you and your children may live.
– Deuteronomy 30:19

Choices are the hinges of destiny.
– Edwin Markham

L ife is a collection of choices? That's right! The choices
you make, don't make or allow others to make for you.
Whether good, bad or indifferent, results are being
produced! Now, if your current results are not to your liking,
look at your choices and be willing to change them. You
must be aware of the fact that your choices are creating your
circumstances and your conditions.

Pearl S. Buck noted, "Every great mistake has a halfway
moment, a split second when it can be recalled and perhaps
remedied." Do you have some choices that need to be remedied? There's still time! It's never too late. Just don't wait!

Don't procrastinate. Have the courage to change them. When you make a new choice, you set in motion a new set of consequences.

One way or the other, a choice needs to be made to either change or remain the same. What will it be? Don't make this choice by default. And definitely don't dismiss it. No more haphazard, helter-skelter choices! Take an active role in your future, your life. It's yours! Don't leave it to chance. Make quality choices that produce quality living.

At any given moment, you're making choices that are creating your present and future reality. So, what does the view look like? Have your choices strengthened you or strained you; supported you or suppressed you? What about your career choices, financial choices, health choices, relational choices and spiritual choices? These are life's critical choices.

Are your choices producing superior rewards or stress-filled results? Be honest with yourself. What others say is an opinion, but what you say is a fact. What do the facts reveal? Don't you think it's time to start making choices that produce life? Why not start now? The choice is yours!

You are the one who must choose your place.
– James Lane Allen

We must make the choices that enable us
to fulfill the deepest capacities of our real selves.
– Thomas Merton

The Choice That Makes the Difference

But if serving the Lord seems undesirable to you,
then choose for yourselves this day whom you will serve,
whether the gods your forefathers served beyond the River,
or the gods of the Amorites, in whose land you are living.
But as for me and my household, we will serve the Lord.
– Joshua 24:15

*When one bases his life on principle, 99 percent of his
decisions are already made.*
– Anonymous

You are at the crossroad. Time is passing, and a choice needs to be made. The choice that can make the difference. Not *a* difference, but *the* difference. The one choice that could change your destiny, forever!

You must know that your destiny is a result of your direction. And your direction is determined by your choices. Which way are you going? Up or down, forward or backwards? Maybe you're in motion, but see no promotion. Check your choices!

If perhaps you find yourself going in the wrong direction, consider making a choice to go the other way. Stop immediately, turn around and go the other direction. It's the only way you will get to your chosen destination. You will never get to the right place going the wrong way.

Robert Frost, famous poet and author of *The Road Not Taken*, wrote, "Two roads diverged in a wood, and I took the one less traveled by, and that has made all the difference." What courage and vision! Are you willing to take the road less traveled? The road that leads to treasure and triumph rather than trinkets and tragedy? Don't settle for less than your best. It's tragic and trifling to settle for settling. Find your road, take it and start living life!

This is not a head choice, but a heart choice! It's a matter of the heart. Your heart! Some will not agree, and others will not understand. But remember the words of Henry David Thoreau, "If a man does not keep pace with his companions, perhaps it is because he hears a different drummer. Let him step to the music which he hears, however measured or far away."

Decide on what you think is right, and stick to it.
– George Eliot

How far would Moses have gone if he
had taken a poll in Egypt?
– Harry S. Truman

A New Choice . . .
A New Consequence!

If you are willing and obedient, you will eat the best from
the land; but if you resist and rebel, you will be devoured
by the sword. For the mouth of the Lord has spoken.
— Isaiah 1:19-20

*Choice of attention...is to the inner life what choice
of action is to the outer. In both cases, a man is responsible
for his choice and must accept the consequences,
whatever they may be.*
— W.H. Auden

Choices and consequences! What you're experiencing
today is a result of the choices you made yesterday and
many days before! And if tomorrow is going to be better,
you had better make some better choices today. But the
interesting thing with choices is that the consequences
aren't always immediate, but they always show up.

You've heard the old familiar proverb, "What you sow,

you will reap." That's still true! If you plant it, you will one day pluck it. Choices are no different! With every choice, there's a comparable consequence coming your way. Great choices are what produce great consequences! Are you walking in greatness? Why?

Could there be some new choices you need to make? Circumstances and conditions aren't quite right and need to change. Don't cower under them. And by all means, don't conform to them. Change them by making better choices. You're just one choice away from a comeback. When you make a different choice, you put in motion a new set of consequences. You can count on it! Expect it!

Success is no different. It's a choice! It doesn't just happen. Make "success" your choice. People who achieve superior levels of success have made a conscious choice to succeed. No matter what they are doing. What about you? You are no different! You can make the same choice!

Successful choices come in two parts. You must first have a willing heart and then working hands. Eddie Rickenbacker quipped, "I can give you a six-word formula for success: Think things through – then follow through." Why not make the right choice and then do the right thing? Unlimited success will be yours!

Man does not simply exist, but always decides what his existence will be, what he will become in the next moment.
– Viktor Frankel

Life is the sum of all your choices.
– Albert Camus

Do The Right Thing At The Right Time!

There is a time for everything and a season for every
activity under heaven.
– Ecclesiastes 3:1

Without a purpose, nothing should be done.
– Marcus Aurelius

Time is a very valuable commodity, but it's often wasted.
It's more valuable than money. Why? Because you
can get more money, but you can't get more time. Once it's
gone, it's gone. Make sure you're "investing" it wisely.
William Shakespeare quipped, "I wasted time, and now doth
time waste me." You can waste anything else, but don't
waste your time. The cost is too great!

What are you doing with your time? Review your
results. Are you profiting or losing from its use? Are you
using it as a tool to create trinkets or treasures? John F.

Kennedy said, "We must use time as a tool, not as a couch." Get the picture! Time is to be acted on, not sat on. You either act on time or it acts on you.

How do you use your time? Do you spend major time doing minor things, and minor time doing major things? How much time do you spend enjoying your family, exercising your body, feeding your mind and spirit and planning your finances? These activities encompass the essence of life. You must do those things that will create the greatest impact on your life. Those things that will make a real difference and take your life to the next level. Ernest Hemingway said, "Never mistake motion for action." There is a huge difference.

Rise above the mire of mediocrity and maximize your time. You can't experience high level living while engaging in low level activities. Evaluate what you're doing. An old proverb says, "An hour in the morning is worth two in the evening." Do your activities agree with who you want to become, what you want to do and what you want to have? Are there some adjustments, some changes that need to be made?

There is a "right" time for everything that has to be done. The challenge is defining the right time, for the right activity, and then doing it! Remember you can not afford to spend major time doing minor things, nor can you afford to spend minor time doing major things. It's too costly! Conquer the "activity" challenge and create the success you desire and deserve.

In everything one must consider the end.
– Jean De La Fontaine

I recommend you to take care of the minutes:
for hours will take care of themselves.
– Earl of Chesterfield

The Courage That Conquers Your Circumstances!

What, then, shall we say in response to this?
If God is for us, who can be against us?
– Romans 8:31

The only courage that matters is the kind
that gets you from one moment to the next.
– Mignon Mclaughlin

Stepping Out and Stepping Up!

Laziness brings on deep sleep,
and the shiftless man goes hungry.
– Proverbs 19:15

You can't steal second base and keep one foot on first.
– Frederick B. Wilson

Wake up! It's time to get up, get busy and move forward. Sitting around hoping and wishing won't do it. It takes action to make things happen. Do you have the courage to take action? The action needed to make your life a masterpiece? A life filled with accomplished desires, dreams and goals.

Take courage and step out and step up to life. Don't shrink from life! Enlarge your vision and reach up to it. Decide to live life at the highest level, no matter what. Don't be lazy in your thinking. Low-level thinking will not produce high-level living. You have to leave your comfort zone. The familiar! The routine.

Never make yourself comfortable in a circumstance or situation that's an enemy to your desires, dreams and goals. An enemy to your destiny! Laziness is the number one enemy to your destiny and your success. Andrew Gide commented, "Man cannot discover new oceans unless he has the courage to lose sight of the shore." The shore is simply the familiar, the usual. What's new out there for you? Are you willing to let go of the old and familiar and reach for the new and extraordinary? Go for it!

It's time for a new beginning. It's time to get busy. Let laziness go and leave idleness by the wayside. They are holding you back from the life you were created to live. And they may even be causing you to become comfortable in an uncomfortable situation.

Don't settle. Step out! Leave the shore and step into life. Don't let life pass you by. Everything you desire, need and want, life has to offer, but you have to step out into life and go for it!

The only things you regret are the things you didn't do.
– Michael Curtiz

Above all, try something.
– Franklin Delano Roosevelt

Taking It To The Next Level!

A man's gift maketh room for him and
bringeth him before great men.
– Proverbs 18:16 (KJV)

Never desert your own line of talent.
Be what nature intended you for and you will succeed.
– Sydney Smith

Do you want your life to move forward? To move to the
next level? That means you have to do something. If
you don't make a move today, you will be in the same place
tomorrow. If you don't use what you have, you will have
exactly what you've always had. Nothing more, nothing
less! This is so simple, yet so true.

Don't you think it's time to take your life to the next
level? I think so. Are you fulfilled and satisfied where you
are? If not, then why are you there? You should be moving
or making preparations to move. Are you? What are you

doing to move in the direction of your dreams and destiny?

Napoleon Hill, a noted success philosopher, said, "The world has the habit of making room for the man whose actions show that he knows where he is going." What are your actions revealing? Where are they taking you? Do you know where you are going? Are you pursuing what you really want? Remember you only have one life to live. Make it a masterpiece.

If you use what you have, it will take you exactly where you want to go, but you have to know where that is. Have you taken time to define your dream life? Do you know what your accomplished desires, dreams and goals look like? Do you really know what you want out of life? If you do, go for it! It's there waiting for you.

Have the confidence and courage to seize it! It's time to make that crucial and decisive move. And you know what it is. The question is, "Will you make it?" Don't worry too much about how things will work out. Just know that somehow, someway it's going to work out. Why? Because you are moving on purpose. And anytime you do something on purpose, everything else tends to fall into place. It's your move and your time. Don't miss it!

You are the one who must choose your place.
– James Lane Allen

The happy people are those who are producing something.
– William Ralph Inge

It's Time To Get Up!

For though a righteous man falls seven times,
he rises again.
– Proverbs 24:16

*Inside of a ring or out, ain't nothing wrong with going
down. It's staying down that's wrong.*
– *Muhammad Ali*

Have you fallen down before? Maybe trying to walk or ride a bike? Yes, we've all tripped and fallen at one time or another. But what happened next? Immediately, we got up, dusted ourselves off and kept going. Why? Because we had somewhere to go and something to do. That hasn't changed!

You still have somewhere to go and something to do. To reach your destiny! So, if you've fallen and lost focus of your ultimate destination, it's time to get up, dust yourself off and get back on track. You may have fallen down, but you haven't fallen out. As long as you can believe, you can break out of any rut. If you can look up, you can get up.

Don't you think it's time to rise up and reclaim your future? Your destiny!

Thomas Edison observed, "Just because something doesn't do what you planned it to do doesn't mean that it failed." Listen to the man who persevered through thousands of attempts to create the incandescent light bulb. He didn't see those attempts as failure, but as results that could be refined to achieve the ultimate goal.

How do you look at your life's experiences? As failures or results? The way you perceive situations determines what you receive from those situations. Learn the lessons, apply the wisdom and look to the future. What would have happened if Edison had quit? We wouldn't have light. The same goes for you!

If you quit or give up on your desires, dreams and goals, you will never live the life you were created to live. A life of prosperity, success, and victory. And who wouldn't want that type of life? It's available if you are willing to get up, dust yourself off and go after it. Don't stop getting up until you get what you're going after! And don't settle for less than your best in any given situation. Get up and stay up! You'll be glad you did.

If you have made mistakes, even serious ones, there is always another chance for you. What we call failure is not the falling down, but the staying down.
– Mary Pickford

Men must try and try again.
– Lawson Purdy

Take Action!

Then Caleb silenced the people before Moses and said,
"We should go up and take possession of the land,
for we can certainly do it."
– Numbers 13:30

Only those who dare to fail greatly can
ever achieve greatly.
– Robert F. Kennedy

What's standing between you and greatness, you and success? And what are you doing about it? Are you demonstrating the attitude of an overcomer? One who looks at obstacles as opportunities to grow up and go up? Where? To the next level of life. Are you satisfied where you are? Why not take the next step and possess your promise? Seize your opportunity!

Do you want to live life at the highest level: where it's your goal to become more, so that you can do more; and do more, so that you can have more; and have more, so that you can give more? What a remarkable goal! One that produces a unique lifestyle and a superior standard of living.

William James observed, "Our belief at the beginning of a doubtful undertaking is the one thing that ensures the successful outcome of our venture." Nothing more, nothing less. What do you believe about your opportunities for the future? Do you have an optimistic attitude toward advancement and life? Your attitude is key. It will take you over or take you under. It's your choice!

Attitude is a small thing, yet it has a significant impact on how things turn out. If you want a different outcome, change your attitude. You must be a goal setter and go-getter. Have a different attitude. Believe in what's inside of you, rather than what's on the outside of you. What do you have in you? Is it courage, determination, faith? Believe in it, and put it to use! It will get you over the obstacle.

If you are an overcomer, you must take action now! Go up at once. Why? Because faith cancels out fear. Take action, take charge and possess your promise. You can certainly overcome whatever is standing between "you" and "it." Don't you agree? Be an overcomer and go for it. It's there for the taking! But you have to step to it. Will you?

To the timid and hesitating everything is impossible
because it seems so.
– Sir Walter Scott

How things look on the outside of us depends on
how things are on the inside of us.
– Park Cousins

Don't Look Back!

Jesus replied, "No one who puts his hand to the plow and
looks back is fit for service in the kingdom of God."
– Luke 9:62

The tragedy of life doesn't lie in not reaching your goal.
The tragedy lies in having no goal to reach.
– *Benjamin Mays*

Everything you need in life is inside of you and everything you want is in front of you. The question is: "Will
you stay focused until you get it?" Charles Swindoll said,
"The person who succeeds is not the one who holds back,
fearing failure, nor the one who never fails . . . but rather the
one who moves on in spite of failure." Will you move on?
Will you keep looking and moving forward toward your
desires, dreams and goals?

Yesterday is gone. Today is a new day. A day filled with
opportunities to make it better than the day before. Step up to
the challenge. Challenge yourself to make today the best day
of your life. Or will you live in the past? Past regrets, past

failures, past misfortunes. Take control of your life! Learn from the past, but don't live in the past. Your best days are ahead, but you must first look ahead and not behind.

The Master Teacher shares some valuable insights for success. If you start something, see it through. Stay until the end. Stay focused on the goal until the goal becomes "gold." When you lose focus, you lose momentum. You loose the edge that's needed to be excellent and extra-ordinary. Keep the main thing, the main thing. If it's loosing weight, stay focused! If it's saving money, stay focused! If it's having better relationships, stay focused! What you focus on grows! It expands and multiplies in your life.

Don't look back because if you do, you might turn back. That's too big of a risk. And if you turn back, you will never be all you were created to be and do. Don't settle for less. Press forward and give it your best!

Men, like nails, lose their usefulness when they
lose direction and begin to bend.
– Walter Savage Landor

You must have long-range goals to keep you from being
frustrated by short-range failures.
– Charles C. Noble

Guaranteed To Succeed!

You, dear children, are from God and have overcome them,
because the one who is in you is greater than
the one who is in the world.
– 1 John 4:4

*Our belief at the beginning of a doubtful undertaking
is the one thing that ensures the successful
outcome of our venture.*
– William James

W hat would you do if you knew success was guaranteed? You could not fail. Are you currently doing
that? Why not? Get started now! If you knew the power that
you had in you, you would not be sitting around waiting,
watching for something to happen before you decided to
live up to your potential. You would be doing it right now.
Everything you need to succeed is already in you. But, you
have to tap into it!

Abraham Lincoln observed, "Without the assistance of
the Divine Being . . . I cannot succeed. With that assistance,

I cannot fail." Remarkable! Do you need some assistance? Tap into it. We could all use some help. He had the "guaranteed-to-succeed" mindset; not because of what he had, but because he recognized what was in him.

What's in you counts more than anything else. And it's not what happens to you that determines your success; it's what happens inside of you. What's happening? Are you winning on the inside? Are you developing and growing? It will be revealed in your results. Release your potential and your power to persevere and prevail!

Mr. Lincoln overcame several "temporary" political defeats to become President of the United States. He never gave up! He kept doing it until he succeeded. Will you? He had already won in his mind and kept running until his physical world matched his mental world. Why won't you do the same thing? What temporary defeat is keeping you from succeeding, keeping you from your destiny? Don't give up! Don't let that temporary setback keep you from coming back. You are destined to succeed. Destined to soar.

Develop a "guaranteed-to-succeed" mindset and apply it to everything you do. It doesn't matter whether you're striving to have better relationships, loose weight, make more money or be the best you can be; the "guaranteed-to-succeed" mindset will help make it a reality. It works! Declare: "I will succeed . . . it's guaranteed!" Now, do it!

Immense power is acquired by assuring yourself in your secret reveries that you were born to control affairs.
– Andrew Carnegie

The thing always happens that you really believe in; and the belief in a thing makes it happen.
– Frank Lloyd Wright

Redeem Your Dreams!

Where there is no vision, the people perish.
— Proverbs 29:18 (KJV)

*Dream lofty dreams, and as you dream, so
shall you become. Your vision is the promise
of what you shall at last unveil.*
— John Ruskin

What Do You Really Want?

So in everything do to others what you would have them do
to you, for this sums up the Law and the Prophets.
— Matthew 7:12

If you want a quality, act as if you already had it.
— William James

What do you really want? More confidence, more
courage, more determination or more success?
Whatever it is, you can be it and you can have it. It already
exists! But first, you must act as if you already possess it.
Don't wait until you get rich before you start acting rich.
Act like it now! You will attract riches into your life. Try it
. . . it works! It begins with possessing the right mental attitude and then performing the right mighty act!

Wanting and wishing for things do not make them show
up. Working does! You have to work for them and know that
they are being created one act at a time. No matter how hard
you imagine the work to be, do it! This is the only thing that
produces winning results.

Success, in whatever fashion and form, only comes about when you take positive and persistent action to that end. Are you doing that? If you want more confidence, you must act confident; if you want more courage, you must act courageous; if you want more love, you must be more loving. It's the only way these things will show up in your life!

Aristotle said, "We become just by performing just actions, temperate by performing temperate actions, brave by performing brave actions." Interesting insight! Question: "What kind of actions are you taking?" Acts of belief or acts of doubt, acts of faith or acts of fear? Whatever you act on will act on you and attract those same things to you. It's just like throwing something in the air. Gravity says it has to come down. It's just a matter of time. It's law.

Are you doing what's necessary to create the life you want? If you want to be happy, act happy. If you want to be healthy, act healthy. If you want to be powerful, act powerful. If you want success, act successful. What you get in is in direct proportion to what you give out. Give more so that you can get more!

If one advances confidently in the direction of his dreams,
and endeavors to live the life which he has imagined,
he will meet with a success unexpected in common hours.
– Henry David Thoreau

It is good to act as if. It is even better to grow
to the point where it is no longer an act.
– Charles Caleb Colton

It's Time To Change!

Therefore if any man be in Christ, he is a new creature:
old things are passed away;
behold all things are become new.
– 2 Corinthians 5:17 (KJV)

Things do not change; we change.
– Henry David Thoreau

You've waited and wandered long enough. Nothing has passed but time. And you still haven't acted on what you want and what you know is deep in your heart. Now is the time, and today is the day. Let go of those old habits, hang-ups and hurts and move forward to a new future. A new beginning! If not now, when? Maybe next week, next month or next year. That's far too long. Do it now! Make up your mind and move toward your destiny.

George Bernard Shaw remarked, "Progress is impossible without change, and those who cannot change their minds cannot change anything else." What about you . . . will you change? Are you sidetracked and sidelined by stubbornness,

refusing to change what you know needs to be changed?
Why not change for the sake of progress and prosperity?
Your future is depending on it.

Look at the butterfly. As beautiful as it is, it wasn't
always that way. It was once a caterpillar. Crawling and
slithering on the ground. Dusty and dirty. Being kicked
around and even stepped on. But one day it decided there's
got to be more to life than this. It changed its mind and
connected with its "champion" instincts. It got tired of
living beneath its potential and below its promise. Are you
tired of living like you're living? Have you been down for
the last time and borrowed your last dime? When will you
say, "Enough is enough! There has to be more to life than
I've been experiencing."

Why not exercise your power to change? If you're tired
of things being the way they are, you can change and make
them the way you want them to be! The choice is yours, and
you have the power to do it. Make the decision to change
and live the life you were created to live. And don't hesitate
because it might just be too late.

Who knows what discipline it takes for a caterpillar to
climb on a limb, spin a cocoon and breakout into something
great? But it does. You can do the same thing! If things are
going to change, you have to change. If things are going to
get better, you have to get better. Make the change!

*The important thing is this: to be able at any moment to
sacrifice what we are for what we could become.*
– Charles Du Bos

*We must always change, renew, rejuvenate ourselves;
otherwise we harden.*
– Johann von Goethe

Are You A Dream Chaser?

And the Lord answered me, and said, write the vision, and
make it plain upon tables, that he may run that readeth it.
.   – Habbakkuk 2:2 (KJV)

Nothing happens unless first a dream.
– Carl Sandburg

Do you have a dream, a desire, a goal? Are you pursuing
something great? Why not? You only have one life to
live. This is not a dress rehearsal. You don't get a second
chance to come back and get it right. So you had better
make sure you're giving it your all. Everyday! Day in and
day out.

If you're passionately pursuing your desires, dreams and
goals, you're what I call a "dream chaser." You've created
an image of the life you want and you're going for it. You're
doing what's necessary to make it happen. No matter what,
for you, it's life at the highest level. You know that you're
responsible for your life, and you've refused to live with
regret and remorse for not chasing your dreams!

Josh Billings said, "Be like a postage stamp – stick to one thing until you get there." Stick to your dreams and your quest for success until you achieve it. Don't let it go. It's still possible. If you don't give up on your dream, it won't give up on you. And the more you move toward it, the closer it gets to you. Take action and go for it! You have nothing to loose and everything to gain.

Don't waste another minute, another moment! Imagine your ideal life, write it down and work to make it a reality. If you work on it, it will work on you. You don't have to sit on the sideline of life. You can get in the race anytime you're willing to get out of the stands. Stand up and step away from those setbacks and situations that have served to sabotage your success.

Keep chasing your dream. Don't loose hope, and definitely don't stop dreaming. Keep it alive! When you stop dreaming, you stop living. Remember that the dream of a dreamer only comes true if the dreamer of the dream really wants it to. It's your dream. Catch it! How bad do you want it?

Dream lofty dreams, and as you dream,
so shall you become. Your vision is the promise of
what you shall at last unveil.
– John Ruskin

When we can't dream any longer, we die.
– Emma Goldman

Are You Living Your Dream?

Delight yourself in the Lord; and he shall give you the
desires of your heart.
– Psalm 37:4

*Hold fast to dreams, for if dreams die, life is a
broken-winged bird that cannot fly.*
– Langston Hughes

Do you know what your dream life looks like? Have
you taken time to truly define it: what you want to be,
what you want to do, where you want to go and what you
want to have? Why not? It's all there waiting to be discovered. In your head and in your heart!

But before you can see it, you have to believe it; and
before you can believe it, you have to see it. What do you
see? Progress and success. Promotion and prosperity. Great
family, great friends, great health and great wealth. What do
you see? What have you been delighting in? The positive or

the negative; success or failure.

You must see "exactly" what you want on the mirror of your mind and then bring it to life. How? By acting on it! You don't need anybody or anything else. All you need is in you, so don't procrastinate. Don't wait any longer! What are you going to do? Wake up to your dream and make up for lost time and lost treasure.

John Ruskin encourages us by saying, "Dream lofty dreams, and as you dream, so shall you become. Your vision is the promise of what you shall at last unveil." Based on your dreams and visions, what have you produced so far? What does the future look like? Is it filled with the promise of achievement and success? Don't settle for anything less than the best. It could lead to a less than fulfilling life. And that would be a nightmare.

Stop preparing for your dream and start living it. You can live your dream and have exactly what you desire. But first, you have to see it and believe it. You can't create in the visible world, what hasn't first been created and seen in the invisible world. What does your dream "blueprint" look like? What do you see? Desire your dream, develop it, delight in it and live it. It's your dream!

It may be that those who do most, dream most.
– Stephen Leacock

Man can only receive what he sees himself receiving.
– Florence Scovel Shinn

Are You Living In First Class?

But seek first His kingdom and His righteousness, and all
these things will be given to you as well.
– Matthew 6:33

You don't get to choose how you're going to die. Or when.
You can only decide how you're going to live.
– Joan Baez

A re you striving for a first class life? Are you living
according to plans and priorities or impulses and
instincts? Know that your quality of life is being shaped by
how you answered that question. Is your life in balance or
out of balance? Under control or out of control?

Are you putting first things first? It will be evident in
your daily activities and affairs. You can't live a first class
life, while chasing second-class substitutes. Pay the price
for a first class life and keep the main thing, the main thing!

Stephen Covey observed that "putting first things first"

is one of the habits of highly successful people. Are you one of those highly successful people? Taking care of priorities, experiencing success and living a first class life? So much is lost and squandered by the haphazard handling of life's most precious and promising opportunities: health, money, relationships, time. Wasted! Keep the main thing, the main thing. It's the essence of life.

What is "the main thing" for you? The one thing that will make your life exciting and extraordinary. It will give your life meaning and purpose. What is it? It's there. It's in you. Search for it and bring it to life!

Will you pursue it with passion, persistence and power? Will you give it the attention it demands and deserves? Why not? The tragedy is that if you don't put first things first and keep the main thing, the main thing, you will probably settle for second best. A second-class existence! A second-class life. Have you settled? Don't go second-class when first class fare has already been paid. It's your choice!

Choose to go first class in all that you do, and you will have a first class life. And all that it has to offer. The extras are included in the package!

Life is the sum of all your choices.
– Albert Camus

Live as you will wish to have lived when you are dying.
– Christian Furchtegott Gellert

You Can Do It!

So do not throw away your confidence;
it will be richly rewarded. You need to
persevere so that when you have done
the will of God, you will receive
what he has promised.
– Hebrews 10:35-36

You can do what you want to do, accomplish
what you want to accomplish, attain any
reasonable objective if you want it, if you
will to do it, if you work to do it, over a
sufficiently long period of time.
– William E. Holler

It's Up To Me!

The laborer's appetite works for him;
his hunger drives him on.
– Proverbs 16:26

No great man ever complains of want of opportunity.
– *Ralph Waldo Emerson*

Desire is the beginning point of all achievement and progress. Weak desires, weak or little results! Strong desires, strong or great results! Is there something you truly desire, something you really want? Something on which you're willing to stake your very existence? If there truly is, I have no doubt you will get it. And you shouldn't either.

Solomon lets us in on a secret. I like to call it "The secret of success!" Listen! He basically says that our desires being fulfilled and our goals being reached are determined more by what's going on inside of us, than what's going on outside of us. Wouldn't you agree?

Sallust observed, "Every man is the architect of his own fortune." What does your fortune and future look like?

You're in total control. You can't control the rain, but you have a responsibility to prepare for it. You can't control what's going on outside, but you must control what's going on inside, inside of you. Do you have "you" under control? That is the all-important question.

The second question that lingers is: "How bad do you really want it?" Good fortune and success don't just show up. It won't just happen. You have to be hungry! You have to want it just as you would want food for your starving body. Do you really want it? If you do, it will be evident in your work effort and work ethic.

Whether it is career success, family happiness, financial success, or even weight loss success, you've got to really want it. Crave it . . . feel it . . . experience it. Be hungry; be driven. Don't stop until you make it happen. Tell yourself, "If it's to be . . . it's up to me!" Remember that your appetite is either working for you or against you. Make sure it's working for you! The question is: "How bad do you really want it?"

Mediocre men wait for opportunity to come to them.
Strong, able, alert men go after opportunity.
– B.C. Forbes

Opportunities multiply as they are seized; they die when
neglected. Life is a long line of opportunities.
– John Wicker

The Price of Success!

But let patience have her perfect work, that ye may be
perfect and entire, wanting nothing.
 – James 1:4 (KJV)

*It takes time to succeed because success is merely the
natural reward for taking time to do anything well.*
 – Joseph Ross

Success is a process. A process that requires work,
rework and more work. There are no instant success
stories. No matter how the media portrays success as an
instant act, it's not. It takes effort, energy and time. People
who are considered successful have worked long and hard.
They paid the price! Are you willing to pay the price? There
are no discounts or shortcuts to success.

Patience, which is probably the greatest contributor to
success, is part of the package price. Being able to handle
the passing of time. How well do you handle the passing of
time? Are you anxious about something; about to give up
and throw in the towel? Don't do it! Let patience have its

perfect work in you.

Henry Kissinger remarked, "If we do what is necessary, all the odds are in our favor!" Many things worthy of striving and working for take time to evolve. They don't happen overnight. Unfortunately, the microwave has wooed us into having a microwave mentality. This can be detrimental to you realizing your dreams and reaching your destiny. Why? Because we look for quick weight loss experiences; instant financial fixes and ultimately, instant gratification. These don't work. The results don't last. They're here today and gone tomorrow.

The things that last are those that are produced in the laboratory of labor. Achievement and success take time. If you sign up for Significance and Success 101, stay until the class is over. Don't leave before the miracle happens, before the breakthrough breaks forth.

If we let patience work in us we will be perfect, meaning whole and complete, wanting nothing. We will have everything we truly want and desire. What a promise! At the end of patience is everything we so patiently waited and worked for.

If you want a successful career, work at it and be patient; successful family relationship, work at it and be patient. Everything comes by work and patience! Be patient and work! The odds are in your favor!

Success generally depends upon knowing how long
it takes to succeed.
– Charles de Montesquieu

It takes twenty years to make an overnight success.
– Eddie Cantor

Finish What You Started!

I have fought a good fight, I have finished my course,
I have kept the faith.
– 2 Timothy 4:7 (KJV)

You must have long-range goals to keep you from being
frustrated by short-range failures.
– Charles C. Noble

It's time to finish what you started! Was it a quest to change careers, get out of debt, loose weight or obtain a degree? What was it? Are you pursuing it? Or does it still remain to be achieved? Projects languishing in the distance? Promises to be fulfilled? Why not break through those temporary setbacks and see it through. If you had the courage to start, have the commitment to finish.

Do you have a finisher's fight? A finisher's faith and belief? U.S. General Ulysses S. Grant said, "I purpose to fight it out on this line, if it takes all summer." He wasn't leaving until he won. Are you willing to do whatever it takes to win? To stay until you see the success you so desperately desire?

The Apostle Paul demonstrated a finisher's mentality. He said, "I fought a good fight!" In other words, he gave his best; he did all he could with what he had. Are you doing all you can with what you have? He goes on to say, "I finished my course!" Basically, he stayed committed to the game plan. He did not deviate from the plan, nor did he doubt the outcome. He knew that if he kept working, progress and ultimate success were just a matter of time. Crossing the finish line and achieving the goal were never in jeopardy.

Have you deviated from your plan or doubted the outcome of your promise? If so, it's time to get back in the race and reclaim what's rightfully yours. Finally Paul says, "I have kept the faith!" He believed to the very end. And that's what allowed him to finish the race. Will you continue to believe and work on your desires and dreams, in spite of the challenges that come? Don't stop halfway. Go all the way!

If your goal is to "finish" the race, you have no other choice, but to finish. Do all you can, stick to your plan and believe. Finish strong!

Never give up on a dream just because of the length of time
it will take to accomplish it. The time will pass anyway.
– Anonymous

The secret of success is constancy to purpose.
– Benjamin Franklin

Keep Going!

She said to herself, If I only touch His cloak,
I will be healed.
– Matthew 9:21

God will help you if you try, and you can
if you think you can.
– *Anna Delaney Peale*

Do you have a winner's attitude? A winner's touch? You're willing to reach out, touch and grab the things you want from life. No more settling! In fact, you're tired of settling. You've settled long enough. For you, it's no less than the best. Because this is what you were born for. You've realized that you were born for more than you have been creating and experiencing. You were born to succeed and win! It's time to seize your success from the very depths of defeat and failure.

What are you striving to achieve? A new career, a new look, a new you? What is it? You've worked long and hard and it seems like there is much more ground to cover. Keep pressing ahead. George Matheson said, "We conquer by continuing." Know that if you keep moving forward you will one day create the future you desire and fulfill the promises you made to yourself. Continue on! It has to happen.

You are destined for your own unique level of greatness. You're just one step, one idea, and one discipline away; but you must have a "winner's" attitude. You have to have the courage to keep going! Stopping is not an option. One more sacrifice, one more step, one more touch and you're there.

We discover a great principle: if you keep persisting and persevering, you're bound to reach your destination and complete your goal. But, you have to keep going in spite of circumstances and conditions. Keep going and don't stop!

Do you have a winner's attitude? The attitude that says, "I'll keep trying until . . . I will not quit." The attitude that says, "I'll keep looking until I find a way, or I'll make a way!" The attitude that says, "I'll keep smiling until I create the sunshine I'm looking for. I'll keep waiting until my waiting creates the winning score. I'll outlast fear, failure and fatigue until I win." Develop a winner's attitude and live like a winner.

The tragedy of life is not that man loses,
but that he almost wins.
– Heywood Broun

With ordinary talent and extraordinary perseverance,
all things are attainable.
– Sir Thomas Foxwell Buxton

Don't Quit!

Go to the ant you sluggard; consider its ways and be wise!
— Proverbs 6:6

Men do not fail, they stop trying.
— Elihu Root

Do you feel like giving up and quitting? If you do, don't! Struggle and strain seem to be part of the success process. You can't violate the process. Life tends to give in to the person who keeps on in the face of adversity and hard times. Is that you? Will you force life to fork over what you truly desire and deserve? Are you keeping on in spite of the setbacks and sidesteps? It's only a test to see if you are true to the success process. Are you?

Peter Brook remarked, "Never stop. One always stops as soon as something is about to happen." Have you ever watched the Energizer battery commercial? The bunny keeps going, going and going! That's how you have to be! You have to keep going in spite of what's in front of you. Go around it, go under it, go over it or go right through it.

Whatever you do, don't stop until you reach your destination and reach your goal.

We are encouraged to take a lesson – several lessons – from the ant. An ant is wise, prudent and diligent. But most of all, it never quits! Have you ever watched an ant in action or tried to stop one? It will go around you, over you and under you if necessary to get to where it's going. Its destiny! What about you? That's the kind of attitude you must have if you are going to maximize your performance.

An ant will not be denied! It will either get to where it's going or die on the way, but it will not stop. Do you have a "don't stop" attitude? A "never say quit" attitude! An attitude that says, "I will not quit . . . I will hang in and hang on until I win!" Vince Lombardi said, "The difference between a successful person and others is not a lack of strength, not a lack of knowledge, but rather a lack of will." Do you have the will of a winner?

Develop the will to win and make a decision today to never quit! No matter what the circumstance or situation looks like, continue on looking for that winner's edge. The winning break! Remember quitters never win and winners never quit! Which one are you?

Many of life's failures are men who did not realize how
close they were to success when they gave up.
– Thomas Edison

We can do anything we want to do
if we stick to it long enough.
– Helen Keller

Do It Until You Win!

Let us not become weary in doing good, for at the proper
time we will reap a harvest if we do not give up.
– Galatians 6:9

*Keep on going, and the chances are that you will stumble
on something, perhaps when you are least expecting it.
I never heard of anyone ever stumbling
on something sitting down.*
– Charles F. Kettering

Are you trying to accomplish something and it seems
like you don't have any more to give? A successful
career, loving family or healthy well-being. You've been
working hard and long and it seems like success and victory
are moving further way. Whatever you do, don't stop. Keep
moving! If you stop, you'll never reach the top.

The pursuit of life, love, happiness and success is still
a good goal! The game of life is still in session. And it's
not over until you win! It doesn't matter how you start, but
how you finish. Your past does not equal your future. Hold

on and finish strong!

It doesn't matter if you win 90 meters of a 100-meter race and still lose. It really doesn't matter if you win three quarters of a four-quarter game and still lose. Who cares if you win eight innings of a nine-inning game and still lose? It's not how you start, but how you finish. Where you are now doesn't have to be where you finish; but you can't give up or give out. You've got to keep your mind in the game.

We are encouraged to keep doing the right thing. The right action will always produce the right reaction, no matter how things look! No situation is ever hopeless, unless you loose hope. Have you lost hope in the game of life? The current score doesn't have to be the final score. You can't change the beginning, but you sure can change the end. Hold on until the score changes in your favor!

Declare: I'll do it until I win!

I know the price of success: dedication, hard work and an unremitting devotion to the things you want to see happen.
— Frank Lloyd Wright

Victory belongs to the most persevering.
— Napoleon Bonaparte

130

Do Whatever It Takes!

To the weak I became weak, to win the weak. I have
become all things to all men so that by all possible means
I might save some.
– 1 Corinthians 9:22

*The men who have done big things are those who were not
afraid to attempt big things, were not afraid to risk failure
in order to gain success.*
– B.C. Forbes

A re you really doing what it takes to succeed and win in
life? At home, on the job and in your personal and
professional relationships? Is there more that you could be
doing and should be doing? Sometimes you have to give a
little more to get a lot more. It's called sowing and reaping.
And the beneficial thing is that you always reap much more
than you sow. Try planting an apple seed. What do you get?
An apple tree. Much more than what was planted.

You will always get back more than you give. It may not
come back in the form you're looking for, but know that it's

coming. What have you been doing? What have you been giving? It will be reflected in your life's experience. If you're looking for more happiness, more joy and more success, focus on doing more and the minor details will take care of themselves.

In order to be a total success, you must follow two key success principles. Do whatever it takes to succeed, and remain flexible in your approach! Are you willing to do whatever it takes? Oftentimes significant accomplishment and achievement require that extra effort. Things average and mediocre people aren't willing to do. The things that separate the ordinary from the extra-ordinary. You must go beyond the natural into the super-natural.

Are you striving for an ordinary existence or an extra-ordinary existence? An ordinary life or an extra-ordinary life? It will show in your zeal and zest for life. I sure hope you're striving for the extra-ordinary because you only have one life to live. At least on this earth! This is not a dress rehearsal. You can't come back and try to get it right the second time around. You have to do it now, today!

Develop a "do whatever it takes" philosophy and remain flexible as you forge ahead toward some of the things money can buy and all the things money can't buy!

I bend, but I do not break.
– Jean de La Fontaine

It ain't over 'til it's over.
– Yogi Berra

Keep Your Drive Alive!

Be strong and courageous. Do not be afraid or terrified
because of them, for the Lord your God goes with you;
he will never leave you nor forsake you.
– Deuteronomy 31:6

*The fishermen know that the sea is dangerous and the storm
terrible, but they have never found these dangers
sufficient reason for remaining ashore.*
– Vincent van Gogh

A re you feeling paralyzed? Unable to progress? What is
it? It's keeping you from moving forward on your
promise to yourself and maximizing your potential – from
becoming all you were created to be and even more. Could
it be doubt and despair? Maybe you doubt yourself and your
opportunities for the future. Don't do it! Could it be fear of
failure, fear of success or the price of sacrifice? Whatever it
is, face it and erase it! You know you're capable of doing
more than you've been doing. It's time to do it!

Don't let *anything* keep you from achieving your desires

and living your dreams. You may not get another chance. And know that you're not on your journey of *destiny* by yourself. You've been given a helping hand. What else do you need? Nothing! You have everything you need. Remember, "There is no need to fear, the power you need is always near." Use it!

Eleanor Roosevelt observed, "You gain strength, courage and confidence by every experience in which you really stop to look fear in the face . . . You must do the thing you think you cannot do." What is it you need to do? Don't focus on your struggle, focus on the source of your strength; don't focus on your circumstances and conditions, focus on the cause of your courage and confidence. These positive emotions are waiting to be tapped. To be released! They've been trapped far too long. Be strong and courageous and take action! Do what you know needs to be done!

Someone once said, "We must act in spite of fear . . . not because of it." Whatever you're afraid of is also afraid of you. Now, what are you going to do? A Moorish proverb said, "He who fears something gives it power over him." Have you given your power away? The power to control your finances, improve your relationships, loose that much-needed weight. Reclaim your power and reach your destination and goal!

One ought never turn one's back on a threatened danger
and try to run away from it. If you do that, you will double
the danger. But if you meet it promptly and without flinch-
ing, you will reduce the danger by half.
Never run away from anything. Never!
– Sir Winston Churchill

Do the thing you fear, and the death of fear is certain.
– Ralph Waldo Emerson

Keep Your Dream Alive!

Joseph had a dream and when he told it to his brothers,
they hated him all the more.
– Genesis 37:5

Dream lofty dreams, and as you dream, so shall you
become. Your vision is the promise of what
you shall at last unveil.
– *John Ruskin*

Does it seem like your desires, dreams and goals are
coming under attack? Everything is coming against
what you hoped for the future. Circumstances aren't cooper-
ating; situations are shaky. Keep dreaming anyway! It's
your dream and nobody else's.

Keep your dream alive! Don't give up on it and don't let
it go. Whether people believe in you and your dream or not,
dream your dream and work to make it a reality! Wally
"Famous" Amos observed, "It's important to believe in
yourself. Believe that you can do it, under any circumstance.
Because if you believe you can, then you will. That belief

just keeps you searching for the answers and then pretty soon you get it."

Don't worry about what others are saying about your dream to be debt free, to improve your health, to gain wealth or even to loose weight. Remember it's your dream! Believe it and keep working on it!

Unfortunately, you can't share big things with small-minded, small-thinking people. If they can't see their own dreams and see success for themselves, they definitely can't see it for you. There are three kinds of people: dream fulfillers, dream killers and dream stealers. Dream fulfillers are out there living their dreams and trying to help you live yours. Find them and spend as much time as you can with these overachievers. They're out there!

Then you have the dream killers. These are the people giving you all the reasons why it won't work, instead of helping you find ways to make it work. There is always a way. If not, make a way. Last, but not least, you have the dream stealers. These are the ones who silently hate you because you're trying to do something with your life and they aren't. You're going for it, and they're sitting around waiting for something to happen. Stay away from these people. They will turn your dreams into nightmares.

It's your dream. Protect it and promote it! It's who you are. Keep it alive and live it!

Immense power is acquired by assuring yourself in your secret reveries that you were born to control affairs.
— Andrew Carnegie

Nothing can stop the man with the right mental attitude from achieving his goal; nothing on earth can help the man with the wrong mental attitude.
— W.W. Ziege

Seize Your Moment!

Ask and it will be given to you; seek and you will find; knock and the door will be opened. For everyone who asks receives; he who seeks finds; and to him who knocks, the door will be opened.
– Matthew 7:7-8

Opportunities multiply as they are seized; they die when neglected. Life is a long line of opportunities.
– John Wicker

Use It Or Loose It!

Take the talent from him and give it to the one who has the
ten talents. For everyone who has will be given more,
and he will have abundance. Whoever does not have,
even what he has will be taken from him.
– Matthew 25: 28-29

No great man ever complains of want of opportunity.
– Ralph Waldo Emerson

Vince Lombardi once commented, "The only place
success comes before work is in the dictionary!" In
other words, work is the way. No exercise, no health; no
work, no wealth. You've got to use what you have. Are you
using what you have? Are you doing what you can, with what
you have? It's the only way you will be able to do more.

Wanting success and wishing for success doesn't produce success. Success comes from practicing success habits.
What type of habits are you practicing? Failure habits or
success habits? Success habits come from developing and
deploying a success mindset. A mindset of belief rather than

doubt; courage rather than fear. Work on your mind! It's your greatest asset and controls everything you do. Use it.

In the parable of the talents, this man had been given a talent and failed to use it; he buried it. He used neither his mind nor his muscle and ended up with no money. What about you? Have you buried the one thing that could transform your today, your tomorrow and ultimately your future? If so, uncover it and put it to use. Remove the boundaries and take off the limits! If you don't use it, you run the risk of loosing it. He lost his; it was taken away. Don't loose yours!

If you have the ability to communicate, then communicate; influence, then influence; lead, then lead. Don't hide it. Provide it to the marketplace, the masses and the ministry. Make a difference. A significant difference . . . in your own life and the lives of those you're connected to.

The miracle is that if you use what you have, you will have more to use; but the misfortune is that if you don't use it, you might just loose it. This is too great a risk to take. As John Wooden said, "Do not let what you cannot do interfere with what you can do." Use what you have! It's the only way to be more, do more and have more.

I cannot do everything, but still I can do something: and
because I cannot do everything, I will not refuse
to do something that I can do.
– Edward Everett Hale

Nobody makes a greater mistake than he who did nothing
because he could only do a little.
– Edmund Burke

Seize Your Opportunity!

The sluggard will not plow by reason of the cold; therefore
shall he beg in harvest and have nothing.
— Proverbs 20:4 (KJV)

Mediocre men wait for opportunity to come to them.
Strong, able, alert men go after opportunity.
— B.C. Forbes .

Are you maximizing your time and opportunities? Or
are you letting them go by the wayside? Take inventory! Baltasar Gracian observed, "The wise man does at
once what the fool does finally." Interesting insight! The
wise person is the person of action, not of procrastination.
Procrastination is the enemy of excellence and greatness
and must be dealt with decisively.

Is there something you should be doing? Maybe planning for future achievement; saving for future fortune or
walking for fitness and health. Whatever it is, the fact
remains that it needs to be done. Will you do it? Will you
seize your moment for success? Remember the wise person

takes action. He takes action now, and considers opinions later. Don't hesitate and miss your opportunity. It will not be there forever!

The sluggard or lazy person will not even plow by reason of the cold. He is cold, but will do nothing to get rid of the cold. He needs to plan, but doesn't; needs to save, but won't. Wasted opportunities! The opportunity is there, but he simply refuses to take advantage of it. Don't let this happen to you! Maximize your opportunities. Opportunities sometimes dress themselves as work; just go to work and work your opportunity.

You will learn to do one of two things. Work in the spring, which is opportunity time, or beg in the fall, which is harvest time. Which do you prefer? Begging or reaping? It will be evident in your actions. You reap exactly what you sow; and in reality, you reap much more. Seize your opportunity and reap your harvest!

The opportunity that God sends does not wake up
him who is asleep.
– Senegalese proverb

He that waits upon fortune is never sure of a dinner.
– Benjamin Franklin

Maximize Your Opportunities!

The slothful man roasteth not that which he took in hunting, but the substance of a diligent man is precious.
— Proverbs 12:27 (KJV)

Opportunities multiply as they are seized; they die when neglected. Life is a long list of opportunities.
— John Wicker

I s there something you have that you're not using to its fullest? You know you're not maximizing its potential. You're not giving it your all! Listen . . . you will only get that which you are willing to give! Nothing from nothing leaves nothing.

If you are going to maximize your opportunities, you have to invest everything you have in them. Tom Peters, the famous management guru, said, "If a window of opportunity appears, don't pull down the shade." Have you pulled down the shade on your opportunity for success? If so, lift the shade, crack the glass and open the window.

Let promotion in; let prosperity in; let health in, let wealth in. Let success be the standard for your life! Abundance and success are there for you. Waiting to come in. They are there shining through the silver lining of your situations. Open up, let them in and maximize your opportunities!

This wise teacher tells us that a lazy person does not even take care of the things he desires and wishes for. You want to lose weight and have found the ultimate weight loss solution, but will not even discipline yourself to stick with it. You craved for a raise to ease the financial squeeze, and now spend more money than you did before you got the raise. Instead of maximizing your opportunities, you're missing your opportunities. Don't let this happen to you!

The diligent person is different. He values his opportunities and does whatever it takes to make them profitable. Are you getting a positive return on the opportunities life has afforded you? Why not? It's not what happens in life that makes the difference; it's what you do about what happens that makes the ultimate difference.

What are you doing about your opportunities? If you haven't been living a "maximized" life, begin today. Start by taking full advantage of today, the present, this moment. And everything in the future will fall into place like a well-orchestrated symphony. Don't miss your opportunity!

A wise man will make more opportunities than he finds.
– Francis Bacon

If you want to succeed in the world,
you must make your own opportunity.
– B.C. Forbes

Face Your Opportunity!

The slothful man saith, There is a lion in the way;
a lion is in the streets.
– Proverbs 26:13 (KJV)

*The secret to success in life is for a man to be ready
for his opportunity when it comes.*
– Benjamin Disraeli

What are you waiting for? It's time to get up, get out and move forward. Get out of your comfort zone, the safe zone. Significance and success are outside the safe zone. Your opportunity for greatness is right before you, but you must go after it. Will you face it, embrace it or erase it? Hopefully, you won't erase it. It may never come again.

Don't worry about what's behind you or before you. That's small compared to what's inside you. Listen to the words of Ralph Waldo Emerson, "What lies behind us and what lies before us are tiny matters compared to what lies within us." What do you have in you? Belief, courage, determination, enthusiasm, persistence, perseverance? These are the only things that matter. Tap into them!

This lazy man in Proverbs looked at everything other than his opportunity. What about you? The opportunity was to get up, get out and make it happen. But no, he focused on the obstacles instead of the opportunity! A lion in the way, a lion in the streets. Question: were these real obstacles or imaginary obstacles? Most people deal with self-constructed, imaginary obstacles. And "fear" is one of the greatest perceived obstacles. Fear is simply False Education or Evidence Appearing Real! If you stay focused on your opportunity, everything else will only serve as stepping-stones to your success. Don't let fear rob you of your opportunity!

It has been said that if you fear something, you give it control over you. Have you given something control over you? It has also been said that too much fear is slavery. Don't let fear control you and enslave you. If you move forward, your fear will disappear! Take action and face your opportunity. You can make it happen!

Know thine opportunity.
– Pittacus

Nothing is so often irretrievably missed as
a daily opportunity.
– Marie von Ebner-Eschenbach

Don't Miss Your Opportunity!

As the door turneth upon his hinges,
so doth the slothful upon his bed.
– Proverbs 26:14 (KJV)

Opportunity knocks but once.
– Anonymous

An opportunity is simply a good chance for advancement and progress. What have you done with your chance for progress and success? Or should we say chances? Success is not really a matter of chance, but a matter of choice. What choices have you made about your existing opportunities?

Alexander Graham Bell said, "When one door closes, another opens; but we often look so long and so regretfully upon the closed door that we do not see the one which has opened for us." What are you looking for? Have you overlooked the one opportunity that will open you up to new levels of living? You will only find what you look for! Start looking . . . opportunities are there!

Look at the door and the hinge that holds it; and a lazy person and the bed he rests on. Quite similar! The door won't let the hinge go, and neither will the lazy person let the bed go. Don't be a victim of holding on too long! The memories of past misfortunes and mistakes can turn into mountains of regret and remorse. Learn from them and let them go.

The bed represents those things that keep you from moving forward and maximizing your opportunity. Could it be doubt, fear or low self-esteem that's holding you back and holding you up? Whatever it is, let it go! You know what your hinge is, your hang-up. It's that thing that's blocking your progress and banishing your chance for success. If you hold on to it, you will never move forward. You will only swing back and forth! Nothing will ever change, and everything will remain the same. Life will be a series of reruns, and you will never see any true progress or sustainable success.

Is that what you want? If not, don't miss your opportunity! Get up and go after it. Go for the adventure, the newness of life. Don't sit down on life any longer. Stand up and be counted. Opportunity knocks. Answer your door of opportunity!

Opportunity is missed by most people because it is dressed in overalls, and looks like work.
– Thomas Edison

How many opportunities present themselves to a man without his noticing them?
– Arab proverb

Turn Your Obstacles Into Opportunities!

Let us not become weary in doing good, for at the proper
time we will reap a harvest if we do not give up.
— Galatians 6:9

*We must look for the opportunity in every difficulty instead
of being paralyzed at the thought of the difficulty
in every opportunity.*
— Walter E. Cole

How do you handle life's challenges – the undeniable
ups and downs that life sometimes bring? Do you face
them with confidence and faith or cowardice and fear? Your
approach and attitude is the single thing that will secure a
successful outcome. So what do you see? Obstacles or
opportunities? Hopefully you see opportunities! Why?
Because what you look for is what you find, and what you
see is what you get.

Hank Aaron, the greatest hitter of all time, said, "My

motto was always to keep swinging. Whether I was in a slump or feeling badly or having trouble off the field, the only thing to do was keep swinging." What about you? What's your motto? Is it to keep on trying in spite of or quit because of? Are you one who will keep asking until you get what you want, keep looking until you find what you need; and keep knocking until your door of opportunity is opened? Keep doing it! You will not be disappointed.

Don't ever get tired of doing what's necessary to create the life you want. If you stop at any point along the way, you will never know what you were capable of becoming, doing and having. You will never know how many pounds you could have lost; how much money you could have saved, how much wealth you could have created. Or how great life could have really been. What a tragedy that would be!

Keep working on yourself and keep doing. You can have more because you can become more. And if you become more, you'll attract more. Step over the obstacle and step up to the opportunity. You'll be glad you did. Life will be an adventure of achievement, happiness and success!

I was seldom able to see an opportunity until
it had ceased to be one.
– Mark Twain

It is often hard to distinguish between the hard knocks in
life and those of opportunity.
– Frederick Phillips

Hang In There!

Then the man said, "Let me go, for it is daybreak." But Jacob replied, "I will not let you go unless you bless me."
– Genesis 32:26

Success seems to be largely a matter of hanging on after others have let go.
– William Feather

Go The Extra Mile!

If someone forces you to go one mile,
go with him two miles.
– Matthew 5:41

If at first you don't succeed, try, try, try again.
– W.E. Hickson

Booker T. Washington said, "Success is to be measured not so much by the position that one has reached in life as by the obstacles which he has overcome." Where are you on the road to success? Do you have the mentality of a miler? The mindset to go as far as you have to go to get what you want? To do whatever you have to do to achieve your dreams? Simply willing to go the distance? Is that you? Are you willing to go the second mile, the extra mile to create your own miracle and make your life a masterpiece?

Many people get tripped up on the first mile. They get sidetracked by the small stuff that really doesn't matter. Don't let this happen to you. This is your life, and it will only go as far as you take it. Be willing to go the extra mile and make it a masterpiece.

If you want to achieve extraordinary results and total success, you have to do ordinary things in an extraordinary way. It may seem uncomfortable at first, but do it anyway. You must do the uncomfortable until it becomes comfortable. You have to be willing to do the extra that will make you excellent and set you apart from the rest. The things that will make you extra-ordinary and attract the success you desire. Why not make an investment in you?

The Master Teacher reveals to us the greatest success principle ever imagined. He says, "If someone asks you to go one mile, go two." In other words, He's saying, "Do more than you're asked to do. Do more than is required." Revolutionary! This one discipline alone will set you apart from the rest and take you straight to the top! Why? Because most people are not interested in doing more, doing the extras. They are interested in doing less and getting more. This philosophy is the formula for failure. Don't be deceived. If you go the extra mile, you will always get back more than you give. Just try it!

Always do more than you're asked to do as an investment in your future. It's one of the many secrets of success. And the dividends are mind boggling! They keep growing and growing and growing.

I am not the smartest or most talented person in the world,
but I succeeded because I keep going,
and going, and going.
– Sylvester Stallone

Give to the world the best you have
and the best will come back to you.
– Madeline Bridges

Perseverance Produces Promises!

You need to persevere so that when you have done the will
of God, you will receive what he has promised.
– Hebrews 10:36

With ordinary talent and extraordinary perseverance,
all things are attainable.
– Sir Thomas Foxwell Buston

Margaret Thatcher said, "You may have to fight a battle
more than once to win it." What a profound statement with such a simplistic principle. You have to keep
fighting and trying until you win. Failure or loosing is not
an option!

What fight are you in or what fight must you engage
again? Could it be the challenge to regain your confidence;
to take control of your circumstances; to loose the unwanted
weight; or save those extra dollars? Whatever it is, have
courage and develop the will to win! Persevere and prevail.

We are encouraged to persevere and stick to the path. Don't stray away, but stay committed to the way no matter what. Perseverance is profoundly different from persistence, yet the same. Perseverance is to continue on because of; whereas, persistence is to continue on in spite of. Are you persevering and persisting? We persevere because of the positive treasures it brings and persist in spite of the negative things that may be in our path.

We must persevere because of what it produces at the end of the path. And that is accomplishment, achievement and success. We receive the promise of success. Perseverance is just a part of the package price for success. If you want success, you must be willing to pay the price. It can't be bargained for a cheaper price. Many have tried, but utterly failed. Whatever you must persevere through is well worth the desire, dream or goal it's taking you to!

If you keep going, you will keep growing. And eventually you will outgrow and outlast whatever is blocking your progress and success!

Great works are performed not by strength,
but by perseverance. – Samuel Johnson

You can do what you want to do, accomplish what you want
to accomplish, attain any reasonable objective if you
want it, if you will to do it, if you work to do it,
over a sufficiently long period of time.
– William E. Holler

Persistence Pays Dividends!

Lazy hands make a man poor,
but diligent hands bring wealth.
– Proverbs 10:4

Nothing in the world can take the place of persistence.
Talent will not; nothing is more common than unsuccessful
individuals with talent. Genius will not; unrewarded genius
is almost a proverb. Education will not; the world is
full of educated derelicts. Persistence and
determination alone are omnipotent.
– Calvin Coolidge

Robert Half remarked, "Persistence is what makes the impossible possible, the possible likely, and the likely definite." Are you willing to keep going until you reach your destination? To persist until you produce the desired outcome? The rewards are impressive!

As you strive for the top, don't settle for staying at a rest stop. If you've taken a break, get started again and keep going, no matter what! It's okay to rest, but make sure you don't rest too long. Time and opportunity are still passing by. The top is your destination. Not halfway, but all the way to the very top. The top represents whatever desire, dream or goal you've set for yourself. How close are you . . . how far away? In reality that really doesn't matter as long as you're making measurable progress in reasonable time. Are you making progress along success' highway? If you are, keep moving and you're bound to break through to the top.

Hard work produces worthy rewards and laziness produces weak results. We are warned that laziness will ultimately lead to poverty. And not only poverty in the financial sense, but in every other sense imaginable.

You can't afford to be lazy in your careers, your relationships or your mental, physical and spiritual well-being. The costs are too heavy, and the stakes are too high. Your future depends on and is determined by what you do or don't do today. What are you going to do? Persist or resist?

Remember the famous words of Thomas Edison: "Genius is one percent inspiration and 99 percent perspiration." Make sure your perspiration matches your inspiration. Someone once said, "You don't have to be great to get started, but you do have to get started to be great!" Get started on your unique path to greatness.

They who are the most persistent, and work in the true spirit, will invariably be the most successful.
– Samuel Smiles

The only way to the top is by persistent, intelligent, hard work.
– A.T. Mercier

Stretch for Success!

Then he said to the man, "Stretch out your hand." So he
stretched it out and it was completely restored,
just as sound as the other.
— Matthew 12:13

A mind that is stretched by a new experience
can never go back to its old dimensions.
— *Oliver Wendell Holmes*

What are you doing to achieve the success you desire?
Could you be doing more or have you settled for mediocrity, settled for things as they are? Don't settle. Even a little
progress would move you beyond your current boundaries.

Why not operate outside the box? Outside those self-
imposed boundaries. Stretch yourself and you'll be amazed
at what you're able to do. Yes, you can do more and should
do more. Go above and beyond and do it! Your new level of
productivity and progress will be beyond belief!

Frederick B. Wilcox asserted, "Progress always involves
risks. You can't steal second base and keep your foot on

first." In other words, he's saying you've got to stretch yourself. Get out of your comfort zone. Life in the comfort zone is a life of mediocrity and minimal progress at best. You must be willing to stretch yourself!

Think of a rubber band. It doesn't reach its full capacity and maximum potential until it's stretched. You are no different. If you aren't stretching yourself in every area of life, you're living a minimized life. Be willing to stretch yourself and become more, do more, give more and have more. It's in you. Stretch it out!

Are you enlarging your capacity and maximizing your capabilities? Why not? If you're willing to stretch yourself, you're destined to experience success uncommon to the average person. That is what you want, isn't it? Uncommon successes in all you do. Stretch yourself! Success and progress is more about you, than anything else. Nothing can deny your success, but you. You can't be denied!

James Bryant Conant said, "Behold the turtle. He makes progress only when he sticks his neck out." Are you willing to stick your neck out for your desires, dreams and goals? Remember: nothing ventured, nothing gained. Put yourself on the line and hold yourself accountable for the results you desire. The turtle may be slow, but sooner or later it reaches its destination. Will you reach your destination? Your dream? Your goal? Stretch yourself and watch what happens!

The men who have done big things are those who were not
afraid to attempt big things, who were not afraid to risk
failure in order to gain success.
– B.C. Forbes

Don't be afraid to take a big step if one is indicated. You
can't cross a chasm in two small jumps.
– David Lloyd George

What You Say Is
What You See!

And God said, "Let there be light,"
and there was light.
– Genesis 1:3

The words "I am" are potent words;
be careful what you hitch them to. The thing
you're claiming has a way of reaching
back and claiming you.
– A.L. Kitselman

You May Have To Encourage Yourself!

And David was greatly distressed; for the people spake of
stoning him, because the soul of all the people was grieved,
every man for his sons and for his daughters:
but David encouraged himself in the Lord his God.
– 1 Samuel 30:6 (KJV)

That which does not kill me makes me stronger.
– Friedrich Nietzsche

A re you going through a trying time? Things aren't
exactly what you hoped they would be. That's okay.
Keep hoping anyway! No situation is ever hopeless unless
you loose hope. It's never final unless you deem it final.
Don't give up. Look up and regain your hope!

Does it seem like everything is happening at once?
Deadlines to meet, projects to complete. Finances are
shackled, and friends are shaky. Personal performance
results are sliding, and relationships are suffering. Don't

fear! Help is near. You may even feel a bit overwhelmed, but don't be overtaken. Acknowledge the overwhelming feeling, but don't be overwhelmed by it.

Instead, encourage yourself and be overjoyed because a brighter day is on the way! It is coming. Have you ever seen a "night" that lasted forever? No! Speak positive, life-producing words to yourself, about yourself and your situation. It will make the difference. Can't you do that? Does it make sense to further depress the situation by speaking words of blame, doubt, fear and negativity? No! Why not encourage yourself?

Motivate yourself and get inspired! I know you have something to get excited about. Even if it's just your expectation for a better tomorrow. Get enthused about your future! Stephen Covey asserted, "Motivation is a fire from within. If someone else tries to light that fire under you, chances are it will burn very briefly."

Look at what you have going for you. Do you know the immense power of that sleeping giant inside of you? Wake it up! It's waiting and wondering when you're going to wake up to the fact that you have all you need to steal success and victory from the depths of distress and doubt. Do it!

Stop focusing on what's going on around you and start fueling what's inside of you. This is when the tide will turn. And you'll know it! Encourage yourself and be empowered to succeed!

Adversity causes some men to break,
others to break records.
– William Ward

Our destiny changes with our thoughts; we shall become
what we wish to become, do what we wish to do, when our
habitual thoughts correspond with our desires.
– Orison Swett Marden

A New Decision . . .
A New Direction!

Whether you turn to the right or to the left, your ears will
hear a voice behind you, saying,
"This is the way; walk in it."
– Isaiah 30:21

Decisions determine destiny.
– Frederick Speakman

What would you do if you discovered you were going
in the wrong direction? Right! Turn around and head
the other way. Take a good look at your life. Which way are
you going? Look at your financial, mental, physical, social
and spiritual well-being and see where you're headed. Are
you satisfied? Don't settle for less than your best. You'll be
sorry you did.

Are you headed in the right direction? The direction of
your desires and dreams? Are you even on the right road? If
you happen to be going the wrong way, turn around as

quickly as you can. Make that decision, now! Not tomorrow, not next week, now is the time. Why? Because your decisions are dictating your direction. And your direction is taking you to an ultimate destination. Your destiny!

A true decision moves you to action and shapes your destiny. Rosa Parks, the famous civil rights activist, said, "My only concern was to get home after a hard day's work." Wow! Her concern moved her to make a decision, which prompted her to act. Her decision, her one act of civil disobedience, changed the course of her life and history. Forever!

Why don't you make a decision that will change the course of your life? Listen to that inner voice. It's telling you what to do and which way to go. Listen and believe. Have courage and make a decision to follow it. Once the decision is made and acted on, your direction and life changes immediately. Instantly! Life takes on new meaning and a new purpose.

Why not make a new, empowering decision and embrace a new direction and destiny for your life? Helen Keller commented, "Life is either a daring adventure or nothing." What is your life like? Make the most of it; you only have one life to live.

Life is like a game of cards. The hand that is dealt you represents determinism; the way you play it is free will.
– Jawaharlal Nehru

You don't get to choose how you're going to die. Or when. You can only decide how you're going to live. Now.
– Joan Baez

What You Say Makes the Difference!

From the fruit of his mouth a man's stomach is filled; with
the harvest from his lips he is satisfied.
The tongue has the power of life and death,
and those who love it will eat its fruit.
– Proverbs 18:20-21

*If you keep saying things are going to be bad, you have a
good chance of being a prophet.*
– Isaac Bashevis Singer

An Old English rhyme says, "Sticks and stones may
break my bones, but words will never hurt!" This
sounds nice, but it's not true! Words can hurt. Just maybe it
should read, "Sticks and stones may break my bones, but
words can break my heart."

What you say makes the difference! Not only in your
life, but also in the life of everyone that's connected to you.
Carefully chosen words can turn cowardice into courage,

fear into faith, and doubt into decisiveness. Don't underestimate the power of your words.

Solomon shares several truths. You are rewarded for what you say; whether it's positive or negative. And since you're getting a return, make sure it's positive! You can't hope for positive results and speak negative words. That's like planting an apple seed and expecting an orange tree. It's not logical!

You are not only rewarded for what you say, but how you say it. If you speak confidently, you develop confidence. If you speak courageously, you develop courage. It's all in how you speak. How are you speaking? Look at the results. They will tell the real story. What you say can mean life or death, success or failure. Are you saying "I can" or "I can't," "I will" or "I won't?" What you say now determines what you do next. Say yes to success!

You are constantly and consistently being rewarded for your words. If you speak with care, compassion, confidence and courage, to yourself and to others, you will create a world that's beyond anything you could have ever imagined. It's there! Create it! What you say is making the difference!

When I was a child, I talked like a child, I thought like a child, I reasoned like a child. When I became a man, I put childish ways behind me.
– 1 Corinthians 13:11

A man sooner or later discovers that he is the master-gardener of his soul, the director of his life.
– James Allen

What You Say To Yourself Does Matter!

From the fruit of his lips a man is filled with good things,
as surely as the work of his hands rewards him.
– Proverbs 12:14

Events, circumstances, etc. have their origin in ourselves.
They spring from seeds which we have sown.
– Henry David Thoreau

Martin Luther King, Jr. once said, "Our lives begin to end the day we become silent about things that matter." Have you become silent about your aspirations, desires, dreams and goals? Or have you sabotaged them by speaking doubt, fear, frustration and negativity?

Just evaluate your current experience! Everything you say comes back multiplied. What you say is what you get (WYSIWYG)! If you want to change what you've been getting, change what you've been saying. Positive self-talk is critical to self-confidence and creative success.

Solomon shares some invaluable insights. We discover that the words we speak create, shape and sustain the live's we live. This can't be overlooked or underestimated. He says, "From the fruit of his lips a man is filled with good things." What you have or don't have is a result of what you've been saying. In other words, if you speak positive, productive and life-producing words, that's what you get in return, but it will be multiplied. What you say is expanded and multiplied in your life experience. So therefore, you had better make it good. What has your self-talk been like?

He then seals the deal by saying, "As surely as the work of his hands reward him." He compares the mental with the physical and assures the same result. If you speak doubt, you reap doubt; if you speak failure, you reap failure. But on the other hand, if you speak belief, you reap belief; if you speak success, you reap success. It's really easy and simple!

Manage your self-talk and maximize your success. What you put in is what you get out. Elevate your speech and you elevate your reach! Be careful what you say to yourself because it really does matter. It's making the difference!

A human being fashions his consequences as surely as he fashions his goods or dwelling. Nothing that he says, thinks or does is without consequences.
– Norman Cousins

We choose our joys and sorrows long before we experience them.
– Kahlil Gibran

What Are You Saying To Yourself?

Beat your plowshares into swords and your pruning hooks
into spears; let the weak say I am strong.
— Joel 3:10

*Man does not simply exist, but always decides what his
existence will be, what he will become in the next moment.*
— Viktor Frankel

Maya Angelou said, "A bird doesn't sing because it has
an answer, it sings because it has a song." Sing your
success song, no matter how the situation looks. This is
what secures the victory! Many people discount the weight
of words. Words have liberated people, but they have also
limited people and their potential to live productive and
prosperous lives.

How are your words impacting you? Are they pro-
pelling you forward or pushing you back? What you say
really does matter! How? It's creating and shaping your

every experience.

Joel shares some powerful principles. First, we are taught to use what we have, to do what we need to do. He told them to beat their plowshares into swords and their pruning hooks into spears. You already have everything you need to be a success. You just need to develop it and then deploy it. Put it to use. What you need is inside of you, not outside of you. You are equipped for excellence! Be it!

He goes on to tell them, "Let the weak say I am strong!" Again, what are you saying to yourself? Don't let your conditions or situations define you. You define them! Take control of your circumstances and conditions by the words you choose to speak. Let your words flow from what you believe, not what you see. Why? Because what you see is not always reality. What you see could be a farce or a facade. But what you believe is the basis and building block for your future, the beginning of your impending success or failure. Make sure it's positive and productive!

As John Wooden once said, "Do not let what you cannot do interfere with what you can do." Use what you have, to do what you need to do, and then tell yourself that you can do it! Then do it . . . it's the only option remaining!

We must dare to think unthinkable thoughts.
– James W. Fulbright

Great things are not something accidental,
but must certainly be willed.
– Vincent van Gogh

You Are What You Think!

For as he thinketh in his heart, so is he.
– Proverbs 23:7

A man is what he thinks about all day long.
– Ralph Waldo Emerson

You Are What You Think!

For as he thinketh in his heart, so is he.
– Proverbs 23:7 (KJV)

What a man thinks of himself, that is what determines,
or rather indicates, his fate.
– Henry David Thoreau

What is your thought life like? Is it laced with positive thoughts or negative thoughts? You don't have to look very far. Just look around; it's evident in your physical world. Do you engage in victim thinking or success and victorious thinking? It takes the same amount of energy, but produces a totally different result. Why not make your thoughts count? They are creating your life's experience.

Ralph Waldo Emerson remarked, "A man is what he thinks about all day long." Think about that! What a powerful and profound statement. What do you think about all day long? If you are truthful, the truth will set you free.

You have become what you are because of your thoughts. You do what you do because of the way you think.

You have what you have because your thoughts have attracted it and created it. Change your thoughts, and you change your life! In an instant. Confront the ills of conformity and mediocrity and change everything about you.

If you don't like what you've been experiencing in life, I challenge you to change your thoughts. Your new results will be mind-boggling. Thoughts really are things! And they take form in your physical world, which means you can transform your physical world by taking command and control of your thought world. Are you going to do it? You have nothing to loose and everything to gain.

You must know that as you think, so will you become. It begins with thought and ends in form. This is why you must be careful about what you think. Guard your thoughts! Negative thoughts produce negative acts, just as positive thoughts produce positive acts. It can't happen any other way. You are your thoughts, and your thoughts are you. The two can't be separated. Take control of your thought life, and make your physical world a work of art!

A man's life is what his thoughts make it.
– Marcus Aurelius

Keep your thoughts right, for as you think, so are you.
Therefore, think only those things that will make the world better, and you unashamed.
– Henry H. Buckley

What Are You Thinking About?

Finally, brothers whatever is true, whatever is noble, whatever is right, whatever is pure, whatever is lovely, whatever is admirable – if anything is excellent or praiseworthy – think about such things.
– Philippians 4:8

As you think, you travel, and as you love, you attract. You are today where your thoughts have brought you; you will be tomorrow where your thoughts take you.
– James Lane Allen

What do you find yourself thinking about most of the time? Is it positive or negative? Success driven or failure ridden? Unfortunately, it can't be both! What do you focus on? Future promises or past failures? Whatever you think about and focus on grows and expands in your life. And since this is true, if there is something you don't want, don't think about it and definitely don't focus on it too long.

Why? Because it's sure to show up.

In his book *Think on These Things*, John Maxwell said, "Your life today is a result of your thinking yesterday. Your life tomorrow will be determined by what you think today." Your thoughts possess immense power. Creative power! Power to create a new you, a new future and a new life. Do you know where your thoughts are taking you? They are taking you up or taking you down, taking you forward or holding you back. Which is it? Have the courage to confront your thought life. It could be the difference between success and failure, hurt and happiness.

One right thought can change your direction and rewrite your entire future. Why not take control of your thoughts and flip the script? It's your future, your life! Why not make it a masterpiece?

If you don't think new thoughts and do new things, nothing will change and everything will remain the same. Is this what you want? A life filled with boredom and emptiness? Zig Ziglar said, "We are often guilty of stinking thinking!" This is thinking that fouls up our future and poisons our present.

You can change your today and your tomorrow just by changing your way of thinking. Think on positive things, things that make a difference and produce positive results. Don't be guilty of casual thinking. Casual thoughts cause casualties! Don't let your thoughts cause you to loose out on life. Make them count for you and not against you!

Change your thoughts and change your world.
– Norman Vincent Peale

What you think means more than anything else in your life.
– George Matthew Adams

Your Thoughts Create Your Reality!

Keep thy heart with all diligence; for out of it
are the issues of life.
– Proverbs 4:23 (KJV)

*Life is a mirror and will reflect back to the thinker
what he thinks into it.*
– Ernest Holmes

What type of life have your thoughts created? Is it a life of fulfillment and joy or disappointment and pain? Be thankful that you have the ability to change it at any time. And not only do you have the ability, but the responsibility!

You were born to win, but even winning begins with developing a winner's mentality. The choice is yours! Your present and your future are riding on your thoughts. What does the ride look like?

Morarji Desai said, "Life at any time can become

difficult. Life at any time can become easy. It all depends upon how one adjusts oneself to life." Your ability to adjust or not adjust is a direct result of how you choose to think. Is life easy or difficult for you? What about loosing weight, saving money or getting out of debt? It's going to be just how you think it's going to be.

Everything begins and ends with the way you choose to think. What are your thoughts like? Are you satisfied with your thought life? If not, change them. New thoughts create new experiences, new realities! Try it.

You must protect your heart and your mind because out of them flow your thoughts on the past, present and future. These thoughts set the stage on which your life will be played out. Watch out for thoughts of self-doubt and self-sabotage. They begin as an illness and, if left unchecked, they grow into an infection. If the infection isn't fought, it becomes a disease and ultimately destroys the opportunity for progress and success.

These enemies of success will short-circuit your confidence and diffuse your determination. Don't let them do it. Keep them out and create the life you dream about. It's your life! Make the best of it.

We are what we believe we are.
– Benjamin N. Cardozo

The thing always happens that you really believe in;
and the belief in a thing makes it happen.
– Frank Lloyd Wright

Change Your Thoughts and Change Your Life!

But be transformed by the renewing of your mind.
– Romans 12:2

The way a man's mind runs is the way he is sure to go.
– Henry B. Wilson

A re you holding on to old thoughts and old ways of doing things? Why? What are they doing for you? Let them go. They are holding you hostage. If you continue to do this, you will continue to get what you've always gotten. Is that what you want?

It's been said that the definition of insanity is to keep doing the same thing and expect to get a different result. Is that you . . . are you guilty of insanity? If so, admit it, drop it and leave it behind. Today is a new day, and it's time for a new way. A change!

Washington Irving observed, "Little minds are tamed and subdued by misfortune; but great minds rise above

---

them." Are you rising above the challenges to your goals, to your success? Maybe it's the challenge to lose weight, to improve your health or create wealth. Why not wise up and rise up? It's all about how you use your mind.

What are you doing with that great mind of yours? Are you maximizing its potential or minimizing its power? Don't let small misfortunes or setbacks limit you to "little mind" thinking. Tap into that treasure! Greatness is one thought away. If you change your thoughts, you change your life. Try it!

Your mind is producing your thoughts, and your thoughts are creating your reality. Who you are and what you have is simply a sum total of your thoughts. If you positively renew your mind, you will release a magnetic expectation for achievement, fulfillment and success. Why? Because your mind is shaping the way you think, and the way you think is directing what you do. If you change your thoughts, you will indeed change your life.

Our destiny changes with our thoughts; we shall become what we wish to become, do what we wish to do, when our habitual thoughts correspond with our desires.
– Orison Sweet Marden

A man is what he thinks about all day long.
– Ralph Waldo Emerson

Your Focus Determines Your Future!

Let your eyes look straight ahead,
fix your gaze directly before you.
— Proverbs 4:25

*It is only when I dally with what I am about, look back and
aside, instead of keeping my eyes straight forward,
that I feel these cold sinkings of the heart.*
— Sir Walter Scott

What you focus on is critical to your success and well being. Your focus at any given moment is determining your direction, which is ultimately determining your destination. Are you trying to do something without getting the results you want? Could it be that you've lost focus? Efforts follow focus! Distorted and half-hearted efforts produce distorted and half-hearted results. What you put in is what you get out!

Whatever you focus on with pinpointed attention begins

to glow and grow. It takes on a life of its own. The goal that you once drove now drives you. You're driven to exercise, to save, to strive for excellence and greatness. Why? Because your focus is now fueling your efforts. The quest to live at the highest level is becoming a reality. In the here and now!

Harry Emerson Fosdick asserted, "No steam or gas ever drives anything until it is confined. No Niagara is ever turned into light and power until it is tunneled. No life ever grows until it is focused, dedicated and disciplined." How true this is. Is your life focused, dedicated and disciplined?

When you focus your efforts and intention, a laser-like energy is created. Lasers penetrate material substance, and focus penetrates misfortunes and setbacks. All you have to do is stay focused on what you want. The same light that illuminates a room is the same light that energizes a laser. The difference is that one is separated, while the other is concentrated. Is your focus separated or concentrated?

Are you looking straight ahead? Don't focus on your current struggle! Focus on your strengths because that's what will sustain you and get you through. Don't focus on your circumstances! Focus on your courage and confidence. This is what causes you to stand strong. Are you staying focused on your desires, dreams and goals? Remember your ability to focus is the one thing that will determine where you go in life. Make sure you're on track to reach your chosen destination! Your focus is really determining your future.

A straight path never leads anywhere except
to the objective.
– Andrew Gide

Concentrate on finding your goal, then concentrate
on reaching it.
– Colonel Michael Firedsman

What You See Is What You Get!

Yet he did not waver through unbelief regarding the promise of God, but was strengthened in his faith and gave glory to God, being fully persuaded that God had power to do what he promised.
— Romans 4:20-21

Man can only receive what he sees himself receiving.
— Florence Scovel Shinn

Go For the Goal!

Brothers, I do not consider myself yet to have taken hold of
it. But one thing I do: Forgetting what is behind and
straining toward what is ahead. I press on toward the goal
to win the prize for which God has called me
heavenward in Christ Jesus.
— Philippians 3:13-14

The tragedy of life doesn't lie in not reaching your goal.
The tragedy lies in having no goal to reach for.
— Benjamin Mays

Where are you going in life? Where are your actions
taking you? People get so busy living they forget
that they can design their own lives. Yes, you can create the
life you want or leave it to chance. The choice is yours!
Know that your decision dictates your direction, which ultimately leads to your destination. Take control and design
your dream life!

You've spent so much energy focusing on where you are
that you've almost lost sight of where you really wanted to

go. Don't let circumstances and conditions cloud your vision of the future. Where you are is only temporary! You're just passing through. You can be concerned, but don't get worried. It's only momentary. Stay focused on where you are going. Don't loose sight of your quest for success.

Don't get caught up in the current events: current problems, current situations, current environment. Let the current take you straight to your chosen place. Winston Churchill remarked, "I felt as if I were walking with destiny, and that all my past life had been but a preparation for this hour and this trial." Everything you've been through is only preparation for what you're coming to. And that's success and victory! Keep going. Keep pressing forward. Don't stop!

In order to achieve your goal of an abundant, well-lived life, you must first forget about those things behind you. It's virtually impossible to go forward looking backward. Those things behind you can't do anything but hold you back and keep you hostage to your past. Learn the lesson and look ahead, not behind!

Secondly, you must pursue the opportunities before you. Reach forward and maximize your moment! You can't live life in "reverse," nor should you live out of the rear-view mirror. Let go of your past and grab hold of your present. It's yours!

Thirdly, you must use "goals" to guide you to your destination. Goals provide direction and focus. If you drive your goal, it will soon drive you straight to your destiny!

The world stands aside to let anyone pass
who knows where he is going.
– David Starr Jordan

Always bear in mind that your own resolution to success is
more important than any other one thing.
– Abraham Lincoln

You Have a New Beginning!

In the beginning, God created the heavens and the earth.
— Genesis 1:1

The future comes one day at a time.
— Dean Acheson

It's here! A new day, new month, new year. Now what? Are you doing something different with your new opportunity? Your new beginning! Or have you resorted to those old self-defeating thoughts and habits? You must take full advantage of the moment. Your moments are creating your minutes, your minutes are creating your hours and your hours are creating your days. And before you know it, life has passed you by. One moment at a time. Don't let this happen. Live in the moment!

Hopefully, you didn't bring those same old thoughts and habits into a new dawn filled with hope and promise. Tell me you didn't. If you did, I suggest you get rid of them now. Because if you don't, today will be like yesterday; this month will be like last month; and this year will be like last year. What a tragic scenario! Is that what you want . . . is that what you've waited for? Surely not! Get busy and start creating the life you desire and deserve. The one you dream about! The life you were really meant to live.

Eleanor Roosevelt said, "I could not, at any age, be content to take my place by the fireside and simply look on. Life was meant to be lived. Curiosity must be kept alive. One must never, for whatever reason, turn his back on life." Are you living on the sideline of life? Why? Life was meant to be lived. Get in the game!

Stop preparing to live, and live. Stop preparing to do, and do. That's when life gets exciting and exhilarating. Is life an adventure for you or boring? However it is, you're playing the lead role. You're the producer, director and lead actor. You can change the outcome whenever you wake to the massive potential that lies within you. Awaken it!

You were given this day to create a masterpiece! What will you do with it? Will you work it or waste it? At the end of the day, you will have to live with your results. You will have to give an account for your activities. Make sure they are worthy of respect. Not by others, but by you. Remember it's not what others say about you, it's what you say about yourself. Take advantage of your new beginning and make something happen.

Everyone has it within his power to say, this I am today,
that I shall be tomorrow.
– Louis L'Amour

If you expect nothing, you're apt to be surprised.
You'll get it.
– Malcolm Forbes

How Do You See Yourself?

And there we saw the giants, the sons of Anak, which come
of the giants; and we were in our own sight as grasshoppers, and so we were in their sight.
— Numbers 13:33 (KJV)

Self-image sets the boundaries of
individual accomplishment.
— Maxwell Maltz

There is a poster that shows a kitten looking into a
mirror, but the interesting thing is that reflected back at
the kitten is the image of a lion. The message at the bottom
of the poster reads: "It's all in how you see yourself!" That's
the question . . . how do you see yourself?

Do you see yourself as a success or a failure; a victor or a
victim; a winner or a looser? It will be evident in your
accomplishments, your relationships, and anything you set
out to do. What you see is what you will be! Nothing more,
nothing less! We must develop an overcoming, success iden-
tity. What you see in front of you shouldn't define you. It's

what you see inside of you. What do you see? Courage . . . determination . . . strength? We must be internally directed, rather than externally deluded!

These men in Numbers saw giants, and we see them everyday. They appear in the form of disappointments, obstacles, setbacks, etc. We must be wise, rise above them and keep reaching for greatness! You must know and believe that you are greater than anything that's in front of you. Why would you think anything else? It will not help you over the hurdles of life and shouldn't even be considered.

Remember you are created in the image of excellence and perfection, but you have to see it for yourself. Strengthen and solidify your self-esteem, self-image and success self-identity and live up to your full potential. Greatness is in you!

Unfortunately, they saw themselves as grasshoppers. How do you see yourself in the face of challenges? Do you see a competent, confident and courageous person? They were defeated in their minds. They had a poor image of who they were and what they were capable of doing. Don't fall victim to this type of self-sabotage. Believe in yourself, in what you can do and then do it. Forge ahead and seize the victory. Failing is not an option!

They can because they think they can.
– Virgil

Man is what he believes.
– Anton Chekhov

Conclusion

If you want to live a significant and successful life filled with triumph and treasure, you must take consistent and persistent action towards your desires, dreams and goals. You must know that your past doesn't equal your future, nor does your present equal your promise. You have the power of choice – the power to create your ideal future. Use it!

All you have to do is place your demands on life and then demand life to hand them over, by taking action. Wake up everyday and work on your desires, your dreams and your goals, no matter what! They are yours. Before you know it, you will be living your dreams and walking in your own unique form of greatness!

In a flash, in a moment, the life you're now experiencing can be changed, forever! Your life will change, forever, if you commit to take action on the concepts, ideas and principles you've read. It has to! Why? Because you changed and every action creates a corresponding reaction. You took action and are now empowered to be, do and have the things you once dreamt about and talked about.

Don't you think its time to move from dreams to reality and from potential to performance? I think so! Nothing happens until action is taken. I encourage you to take action. Act on your desires, your dreams and your goals. When you're inspired to act, act. Take tremendous action. Don't just sit idly by. Act on your inspiration . . . do something. Make something happen! If you act, you will find that you have more inspiration to act on.

If you let it pass by and slip away, there is no guarantee that you will be inspired in the same way again. If you fail to act, you will never change and everything will remain the same. You will never know what you could have become, what you could have been, what you could have done. Is that what you want? Are you satisfied with life and what you've been experiencing and producing?

I know you desire more and want more. Go for it . . act on your heart's desire! Don't settle for less than your best. If you settle for less than your best, you will never be your best. But, I believe I know who you are. You want more out of life. You want to be more, do more and have more, but you just haven't taken action on what's in your heart. Now is the time.

Don't let another second slip away. If you wait, it may be too late. Neither inspiration nor opportunity waits around very long for you to decide what you want to do. It's here now and gone in a moment. You have to seize it and maximize it!

It's no accident you've read this book. Destiny is at work. This is your chance, your opportunity to take your life to the next level. To live the life you were created to live. Remember you only have one life to live. Why not make it great? You were created to excel and live in success and victory. To be something great, do something great and have something great. Ignite the fire within, take action on what's deep in your heart and you're destined to walk in greatness. There is simply no other outcome left. You can't be denied!

For product orders, seminar schedules or speaking inquires, please contact:

The Vision Inspired Performance Group
c/o Arthur J. Johnson II
P.O. Box 682948
Houston, Texas 77268
832.375.0081

info@arthurjjohnson.com

www.arthurjjohnson.com

Printed in the United States
19501LVS00002BB/1-75

9 781594 674310